Notes on an
Unhurried Journey

Notes on an Unhurried Journey

JOHN A. TAYLOR

FOUR WALLS EIGHT WINDOWS

NEW YORK

Published by:
Four Walls Eight Windows
PO Box 548
Village Station
New York, N.Y., 10014

First edition.
First printing October 1991.

Library of Congress Cataloging-in-Publication Data:

Taylor, John A. (John Albert), 1931–
Notes on an unhurried journey/by John A. Taylor.-First ed.
p. cm.
ISBN: 0-941423-63-8
1. Meditations. I. Title
BL624.2.T38   1991
291.4'3—dc20   91-13368
                                        CIP

Designed by Cindy LaBreacht

Printed in the U.S.A.

DEDICATED TO

BARBARA

beside me she walks in beauty

AND IN MEMORY OF

HOWARD THURMAN

who supplied map and compass

TABLE OF CONTENTS

Preface

❧ ❧ ❧

PREFACE

Following years of careful saving, and with the help of a family friend, my Depression Era parents and their skinny seven-year-old moved into a newly-purchased home in the late summer of 1938. The house was the final one on South Macomb street in El Reno, Oklahoma. It, and the town, sat on the edge of the Dust Bowl.

The windows of my room faced south and, not twenty feet from the edge of my bed, was the tutor of my life: a slab of concrete twenty feet wide and two thousand miles long. We called it The Highway: the rest of the country knew it as Route 66.

Through childhood, adolescence and young adulthood the world went by those windows. First it was the Great Depression and the Okies, then the steady rhythm of the Second World War, and finally post-war American which was just affluent enough to be tourists. They were all there: the dirt poor whose gathered possessions confessed their poverty, the *nouveau riche* in their Cadillacs and the old money in their Packards, honeymooners, families with too many crying children, and aged great grandmothers hoping for a last look at a new generation. They were all travelling Route 66, going somewhere, and going past my window.

Sometime during all those years, I learned that the highway was an adequate metaphor for life. "Route 66," Michael Wallis wrote in *Route 66: The Mother Road*, "...will always mean going somewhere." True enough, and all are seeking, as Wallis noted, "a better life." We are all sojourners; there are no exceptions. We're all on the road, some travelling more comfortably than others, some making better use of the daylight, but all are moving down the road. It's the ultimate trip.

During these years, I have been a fellow traveler, and it has been a privilege. What people I have met and what wisdom they have shared! It has been wonderful! By going a little slower and listening a little longer, I have obtained snippets of work-a-day truth, fleeting views of the extraordinary, and the practical insights of everyday people. What follows are notes gathered on this journey: ruminations on the lives, ethics and dreams of those who are more alive and smarter than I could ever hope to be.

There are no revelations on these pages. These are throughts gathered on the common road, and these have always been freely available to any who would slow down and listen-up. It is the usual wisdom of our children, our neighbors, and not a few of our enemies. It is garnered insight from those who are so smart as to be frightening, and from those who look forward to the day when they will have time to read a book. These are the reflections of one who, with you, travels the ordinary paths and believes them to be consecrated ground.

To write a Preface is to write of gratitude. So thanks to friends and strangers who made it possible; to Nimat Hafez Barasangi, Rabbi Lawrence Edwards, and other colleagues at Cornell and elsewhere; to the listeners of Ithaca's WHCU; to congregations who were there when these ideas saw first daylight; and to Barbara who tolerates and corrects the swollen ego of one who thinks that others should read what he has written.

And to my fellow travelers: thanks for what was, what is, and what will be.

JOHN A. TAYLOR
Ithaca
June, 1991

YOU ARE WONDERFUL

I

*When all the doors of opportunity seem
closed and your precious dreams have
turned to ash, remember the human race
ranks first in the realm of wonders.*

Night after night, live and in color; day after day, in black and white; year after year, in the crowded city or the empty plain, the word goes out still and again: "Man was wolf to man." Meanness has captured our attention and agony appears the common portion.

When mothers' hopes lie broken at their feet, when children grow up to be mutations of what might have been, and when sages have become cynics, let the word ring out to the empty and to the lost: You are wonderful!

It doesn't make any difference who you are. With or without wealth, you are wonderful. Those who are brilliant and those who are disarmingly simple are wonderful. The old and the young are wonderful. If you are ill and the days have evolved into restless nights, you are wonderful. Even if you are face to face with the mighty figure of death itself, you are still wonderful. Your gifts remain marvels. That eye of yours which recognizes beauty and grace, that hand of yours which grasps the hand of a friend, that mind of yours which reflects and values, all mark you as the wonder of the ages.

It is easy to forget the wonder of the human race. We are such a frightened and stumbling lot that it is easy to become mesmerized with our failures and mistakes. Yet the knowledge of these are wonders. What other inhabitant of this globe is consciously aware of failure; what other creature is troubled by a lack of discipline or a miscarriage of memory? Even our vanity and futility are signs of our genius.

There are now, and will always be, those who will tell you how dull or useless you are. Do not believe them. The very fact of your being is proof enough that even on this planet of wonders you are a greater wonder. When doubts beat upon your life, and you are pressed to defend your place, remember the wonder of creation which is you. When all the doors of opportunity seem closed and your precious dreams have turned to ash, remember the human race ranks first in the realm of wonders. Whatever happens in life, hold fast to the one fact that remains inviolate: you are wonderful!

Those who would like a lesson in the wonder of human resourcefulness should visit the shanty-towns, the slums and the squalor of the world. Here they will find the most amazing specimens of our race.

Universities, museums, hospitals, and architectural monuments are the usual points of reference for human significance. These, however, are paste and filigree compared to the eight-year-old child who has managed to survive in the garbage dump of some teeming city. Here is an accomplishment of Herculean magnitude.

Frail, unprotected, defenseless, ignored and unwanted adults and children have managed to exist in the midst of filth, disease and danger. These are not, as some would claim, symbols of human degradation; they are examples of human achievement. How wondrous is the human race? Let us garner our courage and look.

What we see is their strength; the same strength which is in us. We, too, are wondrous. We are magnificent beings, and there is a great life for each member of our species just beyond the horizon—on the far side of the slum.

Few of us could become enthusiastic about life if we were aware only of the probabilities. What makes life exciting is the possibilities.

Those who claim that it "cannot be done," or that we must be "realists," or that our expectations should be kept in check are generally correct. Positions of wealth and seats of power are usually occupied by those who pay careful attention to ledgers, who have learned what to expect, and who weigh the possible in the exacting scales of the probable. We doubt them at our own peril.

Yet to hear only them is to miss the thrill of "The Possible." It may be that our dreams will turn to dust, our imaginations may bring us heartaches, and the possible may crash against the probable. But not to know the energy, the vitality, and the charm of "The Possible" is to miss too much.

Perhaps this is the reason that beginnings are so wonderful. It is not what will probably happen, but what will possibly happen, which makes the new exhilarating. It may be that this new life is predictable, it may be that the future is obvious, it may be that tomorrow will simply repeat yesterday—but maybe not. And that makes all the difference!

❦   ❦   ❦

We inhabit a world which contributes a goodly share of sorrow to our lives. Yet this same world also grants a large measure of joy, and it would be well for us to celebrate these joys. What more universal festival could there be than the simple celebration of life?

We who walk this planet, however briefly, are conscious participants in time between two unknown and unknowable eternities. How fascinating and how exciting is this common venture; a venture filled with small and universally joyous events. There is the joy of sharing ideas; the joy of finding the unexpected; the joy of loving and being loved; the joy of having a friend who listens and is heard; the joy of hope which remains though all seems lost; and the joy of work done well.

Indeed, the list of joys seems endless. They pile upon each other until they become adequate to challenge misfortune. If we recognize the common quality of our fears and tragedies, we then should have the honesty and courage to recognize the common quality of our joys.

Humanity is locked together by common bonds, not the least of which is joy. When we have learned this in our bones, our minds will seek the living truth, our bodies may be weary but not bored, and our lives will sparkle like the stars.

❦   ❦   ❦

The change was slow in coming, and miles passed before we noticed that the scenery had improved. After days of straight highways and the flat expanse of fertile farmlands, the family found itself in the hills and valleys and on the winding roads of a different kind of nature. Gradually the monotony of productive agriculture had given way to the less fruitful, but more various hillsides.

There is, of course, a beauty in the expansive farm, but that is a select beauty, primarily reserved for those trained to recognize it. The beauty of the hill and lake country knows no such limitations. Its beauty is recognized by all, and even the cynic must trim his comments. The beauty born of immediate and clearly defined variety is readily acknowledged. In time we may learn the delicacy of the indistinct, but all will see elegance when portrayed in sharp relief.

So it is with our lives. There is a loveliness inherent in the patterns of security and daily order born of affluence, but there is stark beauty in the life well-lived, filled with adventures and misadventures. We may well curse our problems and wonder what evil scheme sends us on journeys to great heights and precipitous depths, but we should also consider the variety and beauty of it all.

Life, like the rest of nature, acquires its beauty out of mighty upheavals and, because of the difficulties in that acquisition, it is a beauty that abides.

❦   ❦   ❦

Today's newspapers could have carried the headline: "NO ONE DIED OF SMALLPOX YESTERDAY." Why didn't it happen? Is the headline true? Yes. Is it good news and newspapers don't print good news? Not true, newspapers often print good news. The headline did not appear because it is old good news.

When good news becomes so common that it is non-news, the human race has achieved a victory. Fifty years ago the smallpox headline would have been unbelievable; a century ago it would have been impossible. Non-news is wonderful.

There is much bad news, and it gets headlines. There is some important good news, and this gets headlines. We can always count on large print announcing: "WAR HAS BEGUN" or "WAR HAS ENDED."

Most of our life will be spent without headlines. Our workaday world is composed of non-news. We may share a considerate family, live among reasonable neighbors, and participate in a community which is about as stable as we will tolerate or deserve. No headlines for us today.

How lucky can we get?

🐞 🐞 🐞

A simple rule to follow when dealing with others is: never underestimate.

This is not to argue cynically that we should not underestimate the evil or trickery of our fellow human beings. The contrary is our aim. Our effort should be to never underestimate the intelligence, sensitivity and understanding of the men and women who share this planet.

Opportunities often greet us, and we are tempted to seek less demanding alternatives. A crisis rises to meet us, and our immediate response is to do that which requires the least amount of effort. Conflicts increase and we, often in haste, propose acceptable compromises rather than creative solutions.

No one wishes to cast his pearls before swine, but are we ever sure they are swine? Might it be that someone in every crowd needs our best? It would be wise, therefore, to err by overestimating rather than underestimating the quality of other's minds and interests. It is an insult of considerable proportion to belittle our companions, but no one was ever insulted by an overestimation of his or her ability.

Our world would prosper if we would understand the remarkable and arduous travels of our neighbors, and then treat them as wise, if weary, sojourners. And, who knows, we might stimulate their journey and our own.

One can hardly glance through the daily paper without becoming aware that a goodly portion of our society is concerned about the quality of life. The public and private institutions, as well as known and unknown individuals, issue a steady stream of propositions which claim to improve that elusive "life of quality."

For the most part, these attempts are unquestionably sincere and often worthy. The petitions to build or not build, the funds to tear down or conserve, and the assemblies to accelerate or retard, constantly vie for our attention. Each supports the argument that allegiance to a particular position will help insure the continued quality of life or assist in the creation of such quality. Surely we need these people and their witness. Without them, the forces of selfishness would destroy the beneficence of the past and the promise of the future.

But it would be wise to understand that the quality of our personal life is only partially controlled by exterior forces, and we are not slaves to the environment. Each of us learns that the quality of life must rest in personal outlook and immediate relationships. This is a self-protection which ultimately saves us from the whims of nature and her various manifestations.

Quality of life, like charity, begins at home. More than buildings or forests, what we believe about ourselves and how we relate to those who are near will determine the quality of our lives.

❦ ❦ ❦

Now, as always, and on every side we are meeting people who are promising difficult times. If this is more true today than yesterday, the one attribute which now becomes indispensable is self-confidence.

It may sound naïve, out-dated, and just plain simple-minded, but what our society needs are some men and women who will speak for old fashioned self-confidence. Those of us who have some gray in our hair and lines on our faces have faced difficult times before. We have seen sickness and tragedy and losses before, and we have survived. It was difficult and we didn't think we could manage the situation, but we did.

We also learned that there was one luxury we couldn't afford: we couldn't afford the luxury of panic, which inevitably destroyed our ability to judge and to act. If we panic, the hard times will surely break us; but if we keep our heads, take a calm look at our lives and assess that which is truly valuable, we will endure and grow.

We human beings are creatures of such talent that the ancient and wise poets could only explain us by saying that we were created in "the image of God." They had no greater praise. None was needed then, and none is needed now. We are no less this year than we were a hundred years ago or twenty-five hundred years ago. Our forebears had the intelligence, talents and experience to meet their difficulties. We have the intelligence, talent and even more experience to meet our difficulties. This present moment does not call for whimpers, but for wisdom; it does not call for fright, but for courage; it does not call for timidity, but for self-confidence.

❧   ❧   ❧

Monuments are raised, buildings are dedicated, and holidays are celebrated in honor of the famous. These men and

women have left marks upon history, and their benevolence will be noted through the ages. One's life is seldom
more than a meager reflection of their lives.

As much as we owe them, however, it is a rare person
who actually bears the marks of the great. Most of us were
influenced and guided by those who were not famous at
all. They lived their lives, made no name for themselves,
died without much attention, and were laid to rest by a
handful of family and friends. The world at large did not
notice their being or their going.

That's a shame because they are the reality and wonder
of this planet. They grew the crops, reared the children,
mended the torn places, and did their best to fill the dark
and empty spaces with light and love. Because of them we
live, and when we sing it is their song which is heard.

Those who were not famous at all lived full lives and
have passed their mantles on to us. We, who are not famous at all, are learning that such a mantle is an honor.

❧   ❧   ❧

It has become popular in our time to divide all living and
all occasions into stages. We speak of life in terms of in-
fancy, childhood, adolescence, adulthood, and old age. Social scientists speak with authority regarding the stages of
learning, the stages of professional development, and even
the stages of death. Shakespeare may have been correct
when he noted that, "All the world's a stage," but our con-
temporaries are more likely to affirm that, "All the world
is stages."

Such has been a considerable benefit to our intellectual
development. To recognize the significance of life's stages
has added immeasurably to our awareness of human ac-

tions and maturation. There is reason to be grateful for such insights.

Still it is more important to realize that our lives are not limited to, nor are they limited by, the stages which others define. While we all recognize such obvious stages as adolescence and adulthood, it is not required that all must pass through every stage in order to mature properly. It is quite possible to live a full and productive life without participating in all the stages that our poor flesh is heir to.

It would be a sad day indeed if we allowed the studies of social sciences, or the theories of some enthusiastic adviser, to become excuses for our behavior. Nowhere is it written that either parents or children must rigidly adhere to expected actions during a "rebellious stage" or a "domineering stage." Marriages can develop nicely without a "selfish stage" or "career stage." Life is not a series of hoops to jump through or stages to pass through.

Each of us is unique—and should stay that way. Uniqueness, thankfully, is not a stage.

❦   ❦   ❦

How impracticable, indeed how sad, it must be to go through life assuming that existence is some kind of sentence which one must suffer, or a mistake which we can only tolerate. Thus accepted and lived, could the costs of birth and death ever be satisfied? If life is but a vale of tears to be maintained, an expanded exam to be endured, we may live a long-suffering life, but one wonders how much fun it will be. Wouldn't it be better to consider birth and death the entry and exit points of an amazing opportunity?

In the final analysis, not to enjoy life is a great act of contempt. Such is to ignore potential, to insult opportunity, and to snub the possible. It is to place ourselves in a position of judging creation and to judge it worthless. It may be that we are causeless creations between two eternal darknesses, and that the trauma of birth and death are high prices to pay for life, but even if this is so, our best chance for parity is to enjoy the accident.

We are, at the very least, earth creatures who can use whatever senses are at our disposal, grasp whatever delights come our way, learn whatever truth enriches our potential, share whatever love reaches our kin, ply whatever trade we are able, and wrestle from the mysteries whatever meanings are possible. Between the forevers on either side of birth and death is an interval, and we might share the benediction of the forevers by simply enjoying this interval.

᭜   ᭜   ᭜

If we blame ourselves, let us also have the good sense to praise ourselves. We understand that there are times when we need to say, "Yes, I am to blame." And there are at least an equal number of times when we should be honest enough to admit, "Yes, I am proud."

Most of us know full well that we add a goodly share of troubles to the planet, but we should also know that, if we have any moral stamina at all, we add a goodly share of benevolent gifts to this same planet. Certainly, we "fall down" and have a right to be ashamed, but we also "get up" and have a right to be proud.

We may be guilty of wrongs, but we are also the practitioners of rights. We play ourselves false to accept one without the other.

When we don the sackcloth and ashes, it would be good to remember a time, and prepare for a time, when we wear the silks.

❧   ❧   ❧

Whether the inhabitants want to recognize it or not, this is a world which has come of age.

As such, it does not ask that the educational and religious institutions supply it with old answers to new questions, nor does it ask that those old answers be shrouded in contemporary and sophisticated verbiage. The men and women of this age do ask education and religion to concern themselves with the great question of our time: what is the meaning of existence? or more specifically, what is the meaning of my life? Insofar as priests and teachers deal creatively with this question they will have significance for our time. Insofar as they offer the questioner some old chestnut of an answer, they will have little, if any, significance.

Our age is aware of the burden of freedom and of chaos. There is no escape. Ours is a sadder, but wiser world. We look to the great institutions, but with a new sense of awareness, and it would be appreciated if ethical and intellectual mentors would not thumb through dusty old books as their sole sources of wisdom. We do not ask that they supply meaning, but that they help us create for ourselves the meaning and value that make life significant and sufficient.

To some this kind of world is empty and terrifying. But we are children no more and, like it or not, this is our earth. It is our destiny. Did we ever have a greater challenge or a more noble venture?

🍎 🍎 🍎

Maturity teaches us that we cannot do everything. There are some accomplishments which will never be ours no matter how great the desire or the effort. Yet, there are options if we are willing to find and try them.

If we are unhappy, ill, or broke, it does not follow that we are condemned to a bleak, dull world. It means that everything is not open to us, but, then, it never was. The options for living, however, are still there.

We cannot do everything, but we can do some things. If life, by its jolts, has taught us where we are marked for failure; it is equally true that life has taught us, by the simple process of elimination, where we are most likely to find success. And one success is all we need.

That one success, no matter how small, no matter how seemingly insignificant, is the key to an unlimited set of options. To do one thing well, and to grow with it, is to participate in a process of living which knows no limits. Every single achievement provides light on the path to new options, to new ventures, to new choices.

All of us are limited, and we will remain that way until we are involved in expanding our abilities. Once that happens new doors appear where only old walls existed before, and no failure, no barrier, and no tragedy can limit our options or check our zest for living.

It is almost certain that each of us will spend our last breath trying to catch another one. The reason is simple: we want to know the next breath.

Life is such an amazing experience that each of us wants more. Surely we can name those experiences we would not repeat. There have been times of terror, pain, and shame. But even if the next breath whispered threats greater than promises, it would be more desired than the end of breathing.

Each of us recognizes, regardless of laments or cultured cynicism, that our life has been a miracle. We soft creatures have moved freely across a stony earth, built shelter against the elements, found safety among the inhospitable, and created significance for ourselves and our kind.

Perhaps alone in the universe, we have lived. We can count the days and tell the story. Our minds, which read meaning into the stars, only begin to grasp the wonder of living. If, when that last breath arrives, we are sad, who would blame us? A final breath, even if choked with sobs, is necessarily laden with an abiding sense of gratitude.

❧   ❧   ❧

It is an act of courage to live when the days and nights of illness have beaten upon our sanity until a kind of haze covers the hours, and we wonder if it is worth it. Courage is required to live when a spouse of so many years is gone, and all which gave meaning, purpose and enjoyment to our days is no longer available. Courage is necessary if we are to enjoy life when the job which defined our place in the workaday world has been eliminated, and the opportunities which were readily available have suddenly disappeared.

It is an act of courage to live when one is suddenly alone and no one seems to care. Steady courage must be exercised if we are to watch children grow up and ignore our careful teachings and destroy our tenderly guarded hopes. Courageous acts are essential when we live in a world which seems to care nothing for the past and which is irresponsible towards the future.

Courage is not as rare as adventurers would have us believe. It is as close as breathing. It is as close as the question: Why me? It is as close as the single word: Why? One would need to be a separated soul protected from life, or one residing innocently in a world of dreams, to live without courage. There are days in all our lives when simply to get out of bed is an act of courage.

Courage is uncommon, but not unknown; rare, but not unique; strange, but not a stranger. Are we courageous? You bet we are.

❦   ❦   ❦

Generations ago, the Victorian author James Lane Allen wrote a haunting phrase: "To lose faith in man, not in humanity." The passing years might change the phrasing, but not the significance of the phrase.

To lose faith in men—and women—and not in humanity, is no small task. When arrogance stalks the world and politicians make narrow choices designed to protect name or face, when bigotry parades as religion, when efforts to increase the common good are destroyed by well-fed whims, and when the good and able are prevented from noble service because of misplaced loyalties or ignorance, it's difficult not to lose faith in humanity. We witness so much destruction, so much useless cruelty, and so much tyranny that the act of losing faith in humanity seems to be the only responsible act.

Then, with a strength which is itself something of a miracle, we lift ourselves high enough to take a longer view. There is destruction, but some still build; there is hatred, but others love; there is arrogance, but not shared by all. Cruelty and disappointment have their days, but they do not have all the days. We see, even with eyes clouded by tears, that people are often better than their leaders, kinder than the haters of the world would have us believe, and more noble than their foolish words or ignorant deeds.

We may "lose faith in man, but not in humanity," and with that knowledge live lives which prove that such a faith is its own reward.

❧   ❧   ❧

"I have never known a bored moment in my life." It was a statement spoken with such honesty and conviction that it could not be doubted. She continued by listing examples of the vitality and variety of life about her. She spoke of the beauty of frost on window panes and the charm in her garden. For her, life had not become stale, and it was clear that the doldrums which strike others would not claim her.

She was not bored, because she had learned to see. At early ages we all learn to look, but few of us learn to see. Looking requires only eyes; seeing demands an effort of the whole being: the eyes, the mind and the memory. It is easy to become tired of looking, but one who sees is constantly refreshed.

The alternative to boredom is not more excitement. Such will be found in the ability to grasp, and be grasped by, the wonder of each moment. To recognize the delicate artistry of frost, the elegance of the garden's most modest flower, or the beauty in kindness is to live the full and rich life. How much time and energy we waste in our constant search and preparation for an expected good life. It is not "somewhere," it is here. The good life awaits us, if we will simply take the time to see.

Here, or nowhere, we find the significance of living, and the answer to those whose limited view forces them to accost friends and strangers alike with the empty question: "Isn't life a bore?"

❧   ❧   ❧

It is common for us to seek assurances that our lives have been worthwhile and that we are worthy. When such is offered, however, we seem to find it difficult to believe the confirmations are true. Even when we are the recipients of praise at dinners in our honor, see our names etched in stone, and gather the accolades of masses, we still question whether or not we are deserving, and how much praise we would receive if others *really* knew us.

We do not know how worthy we are. Others know. They know the kindness we forget; they know the understanding we ignore; they know the care we offer; they know our worthiness even when we are convinced we have no worth. Unless we are knaves or fools, it would be wise to shut down those inner voices of condemnation and listen to those who are in a position to know our value.

When we are praised, it would be well to assume that there is at least a modicum of truth in that praise. When someone says, "Thank you," let us realize that another is saying to us, "I am thankful that you live." Such is not the grounds for conceit; it is the foundation of self-esteem.

Centuries ago, the founders of each of the great religions looked up from postures of prayer and into the eyes of their followers and said: "You are the children of God." Those early disciples were shocked. So are we.

❦ ❦ ❦

Jules Feiffer, the contemporary humorist, may have said it best: "I believe in myself; after that, there's room for doubt."

What a challenge! To believe in ourselves is no simple task; indeed, such seems to border on the impossible. How can we believe in ourselves when we know all the failures, all the mistakes, and all the stupidities? How can we dare to accept such an absurd concept when our days are so filled with laziness, guilt and arrogance? Doesn't it make more sense to doubt ourselves and believe in something else—anything else?

Never. As doubt is the ground from which truth springs, so a belief in ourselves is the prerequisite for recognizing truth. There is no call for vanity here; no cheer for pride. Rather it is a plea that we exercise our potential. Only those who believe in themselves have a base for humility. Only they can grapple with knowledge or grasp faith, can hope and heal. Only those who believe in themselves can doubt enough to become participants in the promising acts of creation.

To believe in ourselves and to doubt everything else is to laugh with the gods, sing with the stars, and breathe deeply that precious vapor which the ages have called the breath of life.

SHOW ME YOU LOVE ME

II

If it carries an expectation of repayment or reward, if it is done out of guilt or fear, or if it is payment on past due accounts, it is not that special act which signifies love.

The word "romance" seems to have little following. It appears that no one wants to come to the defense of romance or the romantic. We live in a technical world where numbers, formulas, and careful attention to detail seem to provide the rewards of life. Who has time for the romantic, the poetic, the sentimental? Who dares to give flowers in an age of computers?

But what else should we give? Should we present a page of print describing this emotion or proclaiming that vow? Would one dare to offer mathematical equations instead of a gentle touch? Have we reached a position of development where statistical proof is somehow more substantial than a tender word? In an age in which hard science is supposed to surpass the soft humanities, we are tempted to believe that romance is as outdated as the age in which the romantic reigned supreme.

That is nonsense. We will gather facts, accept the printed page, prove complicated theories, and still hope that sometime during the busy hours the words, or the memory of the words, "I love you," will redeem the day. We rightly view those who have sacrificed their family and friends upon the altar of monetary or professional success as somehow crazy—and they are.

It is true: we do not live by bread alone. Bread will keep us alive, but it remains the task of Tennyson, Beethoven and roses to make being alive a synonym for living.

❦ ❦ ❦

"Show me you love me," is an honorable request. It is an appeal to go beyond the normal expectations, the usual responsible attitude, and the limited requirements of social obligations; it is an appeal to be "spoiled"—at least a little.

It is a desire for affection which "goes the second mile" when no one asked that it be done, or the performance of a deed which can never be repaid.

For some this may be a gift of flowers, a night "on the town," the preparation of that special dessert, or a few quiet hours without the demands of job or children. For others it will be breakfast in bed, a phone call to express loneliness and longing, or, best of all, a love letter. In every case, an expression of love is something which is special and beyond the normal requirements. It is an act which can never become a debt. If it carries an expectation of re-payment or reward, if it is done out of guilt or fear, or if it is payment on past due accounts, it is not that special act which signifies love.

"Show me you love me" is the human demand that we be given personal and unquestionable evidence that we are unique in the eyes and life of another. It is a confirmation that, under all the chaos of our lives, behind the disagree-ments and projections of a frightened ego, and beyond the pressures of this moment, there is a caring which has not died. "Show me you love me," was the demand in our in-fant cry and will be the request under our final sigh. It is our most human claim, and the response is our most divine deed.

❦   ❦   ❦

They had been friends for more than fifty years. Together they played in school yards, fished the same streams, dou-ble-dated during teenage years, shared hopes, exchanged war stories, and aided one another through the struggles of growing families. Then, as must be true for all, came a

moment of final separation. The loss was irrevocable and a
silent sadness seemed everywhere.

During the conversations which followed, some sug-
gested that the friendship was too close and each would
have been wiser to have nurtured more friends. To such a
remark, the surviving friend replied, "Maybe so, but I
found that I just didn't have enough energy for more
friends."

Here was revealed a basic truth: friendships are exhausting. Acquaintances can and perhaps should be counted in
the dozens, but friendships are few. An acquaintance is a
colleague, neighbor, and dinner guest; a friend is someone
whom we worry about, and who worries about us. Here is
one who shares our life as we share his or hers, and a
friend is one who, by the very understanding of the term,
has a claim on our time and our energy.

Two thousand years ago a wise poet noted: "A faithful
friend is beyond price." It is equally true that faithful
friendship demands devotion which we would not sell.
This giving a priceless gift and receiving a priceless reward
is one of life's most exhausting ventures, but it is always an
invigorating and splendid exhaustion.

❦   ❦   ❦

How many marriages dissolve because husbands and wives
cannot agree on the nation's foreign policies? How many
friends choose separate paths because they are at logger-
heads regarding nuclear development? How many hearts
are broken in debates over political philosophies? Probably
very few. This is not to suggest that such issues may not be
worthy of divorce, separation and broken hearts, but that
public issues are rarely the reasons for personal pain.

Without denying the essential importance of the major issues of our time, we should recognize that our lives are more influenced by the needs of home and hearth than by the international issues which occupy the attentions of the world.

Our lives and the life of our society demand that we be responsive and responsible citizens of the community and world. But it is more important that we take care of those loves and needs close to home which make up the details of our days.

Marriages are more responsive to kind words and tender acts than to breakthroughs in international diplomacy. Friendships are more likely to be built on respect for persons than agreement on policies. A heart breaks or heals in direct proportion to immediate attention rather than political alignment.

After all these years, after all we have been through, and even in this age when some folly may initiate a catastrophe, the words, "I love you," remain more important than the words, "I agree with you." May it always be so.

❦   ❦   ❦

The phrase "I love you," remains, even after all these years of overuse, misuse and trivializing, the most important in the language. Some words may be more popular, others are stronger, and still others have a greater ring of history, but, "I love you, " still leads the list.

These words are the ultimate compliment. "Respect" notes achievement and proves that the honors and acclaim were accurately presented. "Admiration" recognizes the transference and reflections of high hopes as one joins another upon the mutually agreed path. "Devotion" proposes a steadfast support in which all the trembling fears can be laid to rest. But "I love you" means more.

"I love you," marks great wealth amidst whatever poverty. It is an eternal light in all darkness. The words are old, but their repetition is never old; they are familiar, but never routine; they are simple, but never common. "I love you," is the cup of honor which refreshes life's sojourner and renews flagging enthusiasms.

It is a gift, however, which inevitably returns to the giver. To love is an act born of self-recognition which marks the lover as one who is worthy. Both the lover and the loved are exalted by the words, "I love you." This exaltation may be as much as any of us will ever know—or need to know.

❧   ❧   ❧

An adage has it that, "If you want a person to be your friend, don't do something for him [or her], have him [or her] do something for you." A friend is not satisfied by being served, he or she wants to be of service. If we have no friends, we admit to others and ourselves the awful fact that, "No one needs me."

We have made much of the quest to be loved—and we cannot deny this need—but there is also the quest to be needed. As we desire to be needed by others, so others desire to be needed by us. When we reject a person's quest to be needed, we reject him or her. Recognition of this pattern will help account for the sometimes startling responses which result when offers of aid are rejected. Those who are trying to help, like all of us, want to be needed, and if their offers are ignored or spurned, they are ignored or spurned.

No wonder they cry out in anger—no wonder we cry out in anger.

We human beings are tangled webs of needs. We need food, drink, warmth, respect, love and to be needed. We do a fairly good job of meeting most of these needs, but our modern ways are giving us some difficulty regarding the quest to *be* needed. It does not simply "happen" as it once did because the needs of people, while no less desperate, are less immediate. If we fail to recognize the quest to be needed, the human race faces a vast emptiness. Perhaps the question for our age is not, "What can I do for others?" or "What did I do for others?" but, "What can I do to help others do for me?"

❦   ❦   ❦

So much of life passes quickly, silently. Who among us hasn't caught sight of a person in a passing bus or train and, if only for a moment, eyes locked and then—it was over? Natural questions arose: where was she going, what mission called him, what might we have said to each other? But the meeting is over, never to return.

Most of life is like that. We meet people briefly, silently. We meet only once. Rarely is it for more than a glance. Together we wait for the light to change, we sit at adjoining tables in a restaurant, we play at ignoring one another while standing at the department store counter. No words are spoken; we will not meet again.

There is no great lesson here. Just the acknowledgment that we share a spot of earth with the unknown and unknowable. Nor is there a call to suggest that we engage in a continuing practice of smiles or waves in an effort to send happy greetings to all we meet. While such might be a nice

thing to do, there is little reason to believe that these ges-
tures would be appreciated.

With a world so filled with the silent passing of strangers, with days made empty by vacant glances, we might
recognize the loneliness of this planet. This should encourage us, more than ever, to share the warmth of our lives
and the joys of our words with those who are more than
chance meetings. Most of our meetings are hollow exchanges signifying nothing. How special, therefore, are the
meetings of friends.

If we are to seek some softening of hard realities, if we
would answer the world's loneliness and silence, it should
not be a vain attempt to be a friend to all. A gentler, less
lonely world is most likely advanced by being an attentive
friend to another.

❦   ❦   ❦

It would seem that we live in an age of "better houses and
gardens"—better houses, not necessarily better homes.

There can be little doubt regarding the level of comfort
we build into our houses. The technological feats of heat-
ing and cooling alone would astound our forebears of a
century ago. And how they would be amazed by refrigera-
tion, garbage disposals and electric can openers! There's
no escaping it, we do have better houses.

But what about the homes? Are they any better? Or
have we covered our failings as homemakers with an effu-
sion of home improvements? Have we kidded ourselves
into believing that the good life is a color television set and
sixty yards of carpeting? What a sorrow it would be to find
that we are more concerned with furnace than family;
more committed to the mortgage than the marriage.

Many have the better house, and that is good. The trick is to have the better home. It simply requires that we give as much thought to people as to pleasure, and as much attention to feelings as to finances. It doesn't make any difference how shiny the kitchen or charming the garden, if those old dog-eared concepts of love, trust and attention don't reign supreme. Their presence makes a hovel a home, and their absence makes a mansion just another pretty house.

❦　❦　❦

"Tact," as someone has noted, "is the ability to tell another to 'go to hell' in such a way that he looks forward to the trip."

Our continuing, and in many ways commendable, effort to be truthful with our fellow human beings has done little to encourage the skill of tact. Our allegiance to "say what you think," to "be clear at all costs," to "tell it as it is," and to "speak the truth" has contributed to a lack of tactfulness. Fearing that we would be misunderstood, or fail to make our meaning plain, or, heaven forbid, be mistaken for hypocrites, we have sacrificed tact upon the altar which we believe to be truth.

Before we congratulate ourselves on such an ethical stand, it might be well to consider our enthusiasm for such straightforwardness. Certainly the truth needs articulate men and women. There is no question as to the desirability of truth in modern society, and criticism is essential for growth. Still, the vast majority are likely to respond to "naked truth" only after it has been attractively clothed. We may affirm, as we were taught, that "one who corrects me is my friend," but we usually do so with private hesitancy and smile through grinding teeth.

It should be noted that even the Apostle Paul, who faced multiple problems from his friends and associates and was not one to mince words, still argued that his followers spoke best when they "spoke truth in love." Such was simply a First Century call for tact. Even now, twenty centuries later, when we call for truth, most of us still hope that it will come "in love."

❦   ❦   ❦

When death claims a parent, a spouse, or one's child, there are quick and sincere notices of sympathy. We learned long ago about the depths of pain one feels when a family is torn by such a loss. Our society wisely teaches that such an event demands our words of condolence.

This, however, is rarely expressed when a friend dies. Our normal offerings of sympathy, the words of comfort we share at sad times, and the caring in both thought and deed are missing here. It would seem that the death in a family is an obvious hurt, but the death of a friend is a matter of little consequence.

Yet friends may be closer than families, and the pain may be even more severe. Families are given and our love develops out of the years of exposure, common conditions, the times of caring, and the pressures of society. Friends, on the other hand, are chosen. They are subject to the demands of career and goals, limited by the restraints of time, and may be regularly neglected. There is no guarantee that a friend will not move away tomorrow or be lost in the business of other demands. Friendship has no bonds other than the bonds of the relationship itself.

We, therefore, play friendship false when we fail to realize that the death of a friend is as great a loss as the death of a relative and oftentimes greater. To lose a friend is to lose a love which developed from mutual interest and needs and grew to be companionship and caring. We will have other friends, but not like this one; we have others who care, but never in the same way.

The death of a friend initiates deep sorrow, demands expressions of true sympathy, and reminds us of both the pain and hope of that wonder we call friendship.

❦   ❦   ❦

Marriages are rarely renewed by day-in, day-out practice of routines. Marriages are renewed—when they are renewed—when the couple has the courage to "Behold" each other. "Behold" simply means to look again. Those who will take the time and opportunity to look again at their marriage partner and the efforts they have placed in their relationship, create occasions for renewal and the kind of re-commitment which makes marriage significant.

As this is true of marriage, so it is true of much in our daily life. When we "behold," when we "look again," at our children, our jobs, our friends, and our opportunities, we find a new depth of understanding which makes for new possibilities, and gives life a sense of excitement and stability. "Beholding" opens discoveries for us. We see our children anew, our jobs anew, our friends anew, and our opportunities become new. That which could never be gained by unquestioning routine or chasing after fads, becomes possible as we find the eternal newness in the every-day life about us.

There is no magic about "getting ourselves together" or "making life significant." The process of seeing more deeply and finding the newness in even the most ever-present aspects of our lives is no secret. To "Behold," to look again, and to participate in new discoveries, is not a new idea. We've known the procedure all along. We simply didn't like it when people told us to..."pay attention."

❦   ❦   ❦

When asked for his understanding of what it means to be an adult, Sigmund Freud replied: "To work and to love." In these few words, Freud may have provided the distilled essence of education, religion and psychology.

The old story of Adam's fall and his punishment of labor is, in truth, the ordination of his humanity. Work, rather than being a curse, is a blessing which provides each of us with a sense of accomplishment and community. With work we are competent beings and co-creators in the universe; without it, we wander through our days seeking purpose and direction until we finally become lost in meaninglessness.

Love is of equal importance. What shallow and narrow lives we would live without love. Most popularly, love is reflected in the family, but it is not limited to such for no one is exempt from the promise and obligation of love. Love for friends, neighbors and community is a continuing expression of a vital, creative, and beneficial life.

Neither work nor love, however, can alone fulfill the adult. It is the combination which makes the adult; it is the balance of the two which supports life through all vicissitudes. Therefore, it is essential that we practice these: love and work, love to work, and make our love work.

❦   ❦   ❦

The room was filled with old friends, some of whom hadn't seen each other for many years. The air contained the open and congenial conversations which always mark these events. Then, a few minutes after the expected hour, the honored guest arrived. It was his birthday, and the joy was apparent everywhere. This gathering of friends was an experience of love, and its most obvious attribute was an overwhelming sense of freedom.

Some weeks later a few of these same people were gathered in a public room when, quite to their surprise, an old adversary suddenly appeared. It was an accidental meeting. The first emotion was one of embarrassment, then quiet anger and a growing sense of repression. Where weeks earlier, the arrival of a dear friend had produced feelings of freedom, now the appearance of an enemy provided an atmosphere of confinement.

We meet a friend and feel love and freedom, we meet an enemy and feel hatred and imprisonment. We each learn, sooner or later, that we cannot hate and be free. Hatreds, inevitably, shorten our horizons and limit our opportunities. Loves, inevitably, provide us with the longer view and open many possibilities.

Finally, only those who are truly loving are truly free.

❦   ❦   ❦

Love is often pictured as a frail and tender thing symbolized by cherubs, portrayed by starry-eyed youngsters, and celebrated with lacy valentines. Rarely is it pictured as the tough character it often is and more often needs to be. The love which maintains marriages, rears children, helps the sick, withstands the Furies, and does not weaken at death is no anemic virtue fit only for bright days and painless hours. It has the strength of steel and the holding power of bridge cables.

Childish infatuation may be nothing more than an emotional congestion, but love which sees a relationship through all the chaos of the years, through the illness and sorrows, through the anger and boredom is tough. Celebrating a birth or embracing a smiling and freshly diapered infant may be a study in sentimentality, but the years of diapers, the nights of gnawing fear, the disappointments and frustration of exhausted and caring parents confess that love is tough. Occasional references to "Dear old Mom" or "Dear old Dad" may be exercises in nostalgia which parade as love, but to honor father and mother through their mistakes and failures, to watch age take its inevitable toll and not lose the sense of respect, to meet illness and the loss of faculties with a mind that remembers and a kiss that cares is tough love. To stand alongside a friend whom the rest of the community has abandoned, to honor a neighbor with kindness and respect, to criticize a nation and not abandon it, to give without expectation of repayment or even recognition, are all examples of a love whose will is as an oak tree and whose endurance is as granite.

Love blesses marriages, rears children, builds civilizations, lifts the fallen, and emboldens life. Love, whatever else it may be, is tough.

Someone wrote, "Politeness is love in action." If that is so, and it makes much sense, then love is a far more visible virtue than was suspected. Love becomes more than a verb, a passing greeting, or an ancient ideal, it becomes the continuing interaction between people.

Our communities are not short of those who claim to practice the love ethic. Certainly there is no shortage of pronouncements, politicians and preachers who affirm the value of love. But how is it witnessed? How visible is our love?

No law demands that a door be held open while another approaches, no religion requires the courtesies which make driving an automobile a less hazardous adventure, no local ordinance makes the gracious words "Please" and "Thanks" obligatory, and no ruling dictates words of kindness or notes of appreciation. These are self-imposed expressions of politeness.

Our days are often filled with stress, and weighty issues press upon us. It is easy to excuse our sharp words and scrambling instances of impoliteness. But the fact remains that the seconds spent, or not spent, in some polite act reveal more about our belief in love than all our high-flown praises or our many declarations on appropriate altars. It is easy to believe in love; the rub comes in doing it.

If politeness is love in action then love is directly practical, and the question "How's your love life?" becomes immediately relevant.

❦   ❦   ❦

One of the liabilities of our lives and that of our society is the confusion between the adjectives famous and important. We live in a world, and at a time, when the words threaten to become synonyms. They are not.

In the age of instant world-wide communication, we are readily confronted with famous people. It is tempting to assume that they are important to us. But the leader of a nation, a gathering of a distant population, or the discovery of new wealth may enable people to become famous: it does not necessarily follow that they are important. In truth, these people labeled "important" may be incidental to our lives. In rare cases, the famous may be of material interest to us, but it is more likely that the famous will only become important if we choose to make them so.

Those who are important are usually very close. We know the truly important by their first names, or by their relationship to our lives. They have earned their place by their significant and often continuing effect upon us. Their deeds have made us what we are, their ideas and hopes influence our thoughts, and their words make or break our days. What folly it is to believe that the famous are important. They are but shadows and echoes, and not to be confused with the child, the friend, the physician, the mechanic—those who are really important.

❦ ❦ ❦

There was a time, and not too long ago, when wedding vows were all the same. Each bride and each groom knew that they were going to say something about loving and honoring, and that the bride would promise to obey. How things and times have changed! First, brides were driven by a growing sense of self-esteem to denounce the obedience pledge. Once that was dismissed, other revisions followed.

Now it is not unusual for the couple to prepare their own vows based upon their understanding of the lifetime commitment. Often these new vows contain a statement to the effect that they will not only be husband and wife, but will also be each other's best friend.

This should not be taken lightly. Marriage, if it is no more than a binding agreement sanctioned by religion and state, may become a prison. If the husband and wife are bound only by affection born of courtship, a marriage can threaten to become sentimental. But if the couple finds that their relationship is a bond recognized by the public, a love born of attraction and passion, and also complemented by friendship, a marriage may very well be built upon a rock.

For a husband and wife to be one another's best friend is to participate in a voluntary union of honor. Friendship is both a high compliment and a noble obligation. A friend hears confessions and administers the balm of understanding and care. A friend is close enough to heal for, as the author of Ecclesiasticus wrote: "A faithful friend is life-giving medicine." Who could ask more—or less—of a spouse?

❦   ❦   ❦

Sincere and honest differences of opinion do not always shatter friendships, they may reinforce them.

Each of us knows of long-time friendships which have been fractured on the stormy sea of controversy. Few are those who could not tell a story of friends who were closer than family, but were torn asunder by some issue of significance. A sadness ripples through the community when these people go their separate ways, and it seems that all friendships are shaken.

We, however, should ask ourselves about the validity and strength of such a friendship. Are friends only those who share constant agreements? Isn't there room for differing opinions?

Friends are those who appreciate each other enough to allow disagreements. They do not base their friendship on the control of another's ideas and opinions. Good friends recognize that they will hold differing views on controversial issues, and further recognize that such differences are public notices of the strength of their relationship. These people understand that there will be some table-pounding, door-slamming arguments, but these arguments only validate the willingness for each to be his or her own person.

True friendship urges honesty as well as concern; it invites differences as well as similarities; it encourages exchanges as well as compliments.

❧   ❧   ❧

The summer afternoon was sunny and the young couple faced each other in the midst of a well-kept garden and were surrounded by friends as they repeated their marriage vows. Those vows, in part, were: "Loving what I know; trusting what I do not know."

Herein lies the essence of human relationships. To love what one knows is to give another the supreme compliment; that is, to accept, appreciate and nurture what is recognized. But the second part of the vow may be more important: to trust what is not known. Surely we honor love, but trusting is essential to the marriage and, for that matter, to all relationships.

When other human qualities have been analyzed, computerized and bureaucratized, trust will remain. Trust lives beyond rules and regulations, it is stronger than bonds of sentiment, and it stands straight long after the vitality of early love has failed. It is the tender pledge on a wedding day, and it is the single foundation of peace between nations. With it our individual lives can meet any manner of obstacles; without it even civilizations quake at minimal disturbances.

Trusting what we cannot know gives witness to the mystery which is embedded deeply into our private lives and the ways of nations, and it affirms those mysteries as honest and healthy. To trust is to honor another's secret treasury with full knowledge that we will never visit such a place—and there is no need to.

❦   ❦   ❦

The mother was at her wit's end. The children had exhausted the last shred of patience. What was she to do and, moreover, how were the children to know that she loved them?

The young couple were talented and committed, but the careers demanded so much, and there was so little time. The silent question seemed omnipresent, "Am I still loved?"

Wedding anniversaries were too many to be remembered, and the couple had long ago learned the necessary art of taking, and being taken, for granted. Yet how were they to know that the other was so very much in love?

We are parents who are rearing responsible adults for a challenging society. We are caring people making our way in a world with demands and defeats on every side. We are the ones who know that being taken for granted is the stuff of faithfulness. Still the longing to know that we are loved and lovable remain. Without such an awareness all of us are lonely, empty, and frightened.

Parents, children, friends, relations, spouses, we do indeed love them. But how do they know we love them? What proofs may be offered? And especially, what proofs shall we offer before this day ends?

❦   ❦   ❦

It is reported that observers of the early Christian faith exclaimed: "See how these Christians love one another." There is no way to prove that such was actually said, that the remark was an accurate description of Jesus' followers, or even if the Christians did indeed love one another. But most would like to believe that it was so.

Our desire to believe rests in the simple hope that there was a time when a community of men and women, boys and girls, did love one another. Our age seems to be so filled with tension and fears, with caution and sophistication, that we are unlikely to love many. While such a relationship might have existed at another time, it is not expected in our lives. We are too hesitant, too shy, and too stoic to love more than a few.

We, however, can trust one another. In an angry, frightened and litigious society, this is no simple task. Trust is the basis of friendship, the foundation of marriage, the security of families, the lubricant of worthy institutions, and the tie which makes civilization possible. Without it, our world is worse than a jungle.

It may be that we will not love one another, but at least we can do the next best thing.

It was a polite conversation, and we were asking the polite questions. "Where do you live?" I inquired. "North of here," he replied, "where I could find a place for my dog." His final remark before going about his business was: "Home is where my dog is."

Home is where his dog is? What kind of statement is that? Certainly, it was a new one! We've all heard: "Home is where I grew up," or "Home is where my family is," or even "Home is anywhere I hang my hat." But "Home is where my dog is"?

After a few moments of reflection his statement didn't seem so strange. Home is, or should be, where we feel most comfortable, and where we love and are loved. For this young man, he most experienced love through his relationship with his dog and, therefore, home was where his dog was.

When we begin to examine the situation, it becomes apparent that the young man was revealing a truth. It's not the house, or yard, or neighborhood which makes it home. It's love, care and being there with someone or something. Without these a house is a building, a family is a group, and a pet is a nuisance.

Home, finally and for each of us, is where love is.

WHAT DO YOU SAY TO A HIPPOPOTAMUS?

III

When we experience something new,
fascinating or frightening, the first thing
required is to term the experience correctly.

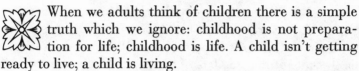 When we adults think of children there is a simple truth which we ignore: childhood is not preparation for life; childhood is life. A child isn't getting ready to live; a child is living.

Children are constantly confronted with the nagging question: "What are you going to be?" Courageous would be the youngster who, looking the adult squarely in the face, would say, "I'm not going to be anything; I already am." We adults would be shocked by such an insolent remark, for we have forgotten, if indeed we ever knew, that a child is an active, participating and contributing member of society from the time of birth. Childhood isn't a time when a pre-human is molded into a human who will then live life; the child is a human who is living life. No child will miss the zest and joy of living unless these are denied by adults who have convinced themselves that childhood is a period of preparation.

How much heartache we would save ourselves if we would recognize children as partners with adults in the process of living, rather than always viewing them as apprentices. How much we could teach each other; we have the experience and they have the freshness. How full both our lives could be.

The children may not lead us, but at least we ought to discuss the trip with them, for, after all, life is their journey, too.

❧ ❧ ❧

The vacation was a grand success, and everyone had a wonderful time, yet the suitcases will not be put down before someone is sure to say, "It's good to be back home." This can be, one supposes, a type of familial ritual which is designed to reduce the essential disappointment of returning to the accustomed tasks, or an effort to keep some member of the family happy, but usually it's more authentic. In spite of the wonders of travel and the benefits of diversity, most of us still find something intrinsically rewarding about returning home.

There is, of course, the contentment which comes from recognizing the familiar. Chairs in their usual places, photographs recognized in customary spots, caring voices on the phone, and the preferred—our very own—bed, all go to affirm our welcome. The reality that waiting tasks still face us, that the vacation magic did nothing to reduce the continuing problems, and that marching time exposed new sorrows, do not dim the blessings of the return. It is good to get away, and it is good, maybe even better, to get back.

One of the consequences of returning—and the one which may make going most worthwhile—is to see that which had grown commonplace, now with a more attentive vision. New appreciations arise, fresh understandings of the usual come into focus, that which had become dull now fairly glistens with vitality, and home becomes HOME. "Welcome back" and "It's good to be back" must be listed among our finest exchanges.

"I want to go home," is not simply a child's whine; it is a human condition which makes the act of returning a celebration.

❦   ❦   ❦

The Biblical parable of The Prodigal Son has many subtleties, and it conveys a variety of lessons. But there is one obvious and inescapable message: Nothing can separate the offspring from the parent's love.

Unfortunately, the popularity and simplicity of the message have some difficulty being translated into our lives. Hardly a day goes by when we are not confronted with some new example of a child's separation from the father's or mother's love, or children separated from their parents' love. The reasons for such separations are ever at hand: failure, behavior, friends, drugs, and much more. It has become fashionable to claim that children must rebel and be separated.

The old lesson, however, remains. One can't help wondering how much improved this world might be if parents conveyed to their children, in both words and actions, the simple message of the parable: "No matter what you do or how you act or what you say, I will love you." We might go on to say that we may not approve of their ways, but approval is not prerequisite to love.

Parents are often concerned with factors over which they have no control: their children's abilities, their friends, and the social environment. Perhaps parents would fare better if they paid more attention to the one element over which they do have control: their love for their children.

The father in the parable could not control his son's rebellion, but he could love his child and welcome him home. And that's all that really mattered.

❧ ❧ ❧

The boy was nearly eleven and the grandfather over sixty, and their conversation was directed to one of the weightier problems. This afternoon's discussion concerned the speed of time. The boy said, "The years go by too slowly and this year seems very long." The older man answered quickly, "Years pass slowly only for the young."

Surely there are years which pass ever so slowly for some adults, but these are exceptions. Most of us find the years speeding before our eyes.

Why? Is it only because the inevitable figure of death waits and seems to grow larger as the years pass? Perhaps, but probably not. It is more likely that the years seem brief because our understanding of their gifts increases. The child may recognize only the drudgery of school and the boredom of played-out toys. But the aging adults, whether they be thirty or ninety, understand that each galloping year is a depository of cherished memories and challenging hopes.

Years pass rapidly, not because of their scarcity, but because they are packed with life's values. The achievements, honors, loves, joys, and even the tragedies give each year a worthiness which cannot be duplicated or depreciated.

Maturity, as the young boy will learn, is simply a recognition of life's value. If we grow old and do not learn this, we grow old in vain.

❦   ❦   ❦

How easy it is to get along with people when everyone is happy, and how difficult life becomes when unhappiness abounds. It, therefore, is natural that we hold fast to the pleasant feelings and evade the difficult times.

In spite of our good intentions, however, we cannot always maintain qualities of gentleness and consideration. Each of us experiences moments when the strains reach the breaking point and anger tears through. Sometimes this anger takes the form of a word or many words, or a look, or even a disgusted and disgusting moment. These are not our better times, but they are human and should be recognized as such.

Unfortunately, our angry outbursts are often directed at innocent victims. As a result, they are hurt, and we are embarrassed. There is good reason for both reactions. What has happened is unpleasant even though it is very natural.

Anger often arises in the midst of family or friends because that is the environment in which we feel most honest. We should not need to play games of "let's pretend" with those we love. If we must be angry, then let us be angry within those environments where our anger is both accepted and understood, and where love and decency keep it within bounds.

Each of us needs those who will share our difficult moments as well as our charming ones. To accept each other, warts and all, is the final testament of love.

❦   ❦   ❦

It might be helpful if we adults could appreciate that a child has the right kind and amount of intelligence for a child. A child's intelligence, his or her view of the world, is exactly right for him or her. In that simple statement lie many of the problems which have been grouped under the heading: "Generation Gap."

Of course there is a gap...and there should be. If it is foolish for an adult to think like a child, it is equally foolish for a child to think like an adult. A child has the intelligence to survive in a child's world. Adult intelligence wouldn't stand a chance. What adult among us could weather either the naïveté or the brutality of the child's everyday environment? The natural aptitude we enjoyed in childhood has been replaced by the awareness which is natural for an adult, and we can no more regain our childhood mental agility than we can regain our childhood physical agility.

This is not to say a child's intelligence is better than an adult's, only different. If we adults recognize this, we may rid ourselves of the obsessive desire to transform our children into "little men" or "little women," and allow them the natural wit and defense which belongs to them.

In due time, the child's intelligence will mature. If the adults who are close to this child have been "adult smart" and "adult loving" enough, that mature intelligence may look a lot like wisdom.

❦   ❦   ❦

It was a common situation, repeated thousands of times in hundreds of cities: a grandfather escorting his grandson through the maze of a zoo.

They were moving from exhibit to exhibit when they came to the special water and beach enclosure built for hippopotamuses. The child, fascinated by the giant creatures with their huge mouths, turned to his companion and asked: "Grandpa, what do you say to a hippopotamus?"

"I don't know," the grandfather replied, "but I guess you'd just say, 'Hello, Hippopotamus.'"

We are far more sophisticated than the child. Our questions and answers are more complex. Nevertheless, this vignette has a lesson for us all. When we meet an experience which is new, fascinating or frightening, the first thing required is to term the experience correctly.

What do we say to a hippopotamus? We say, "Hello, Hippopotamus." We do not say, "Hello, Elephant," or "Hello, Man" or "Hello, Rock." We see a hippopotamus, and we call it a hippopotamus. We would save ourselves much difficulty by following that example. Trouble is "trouble," defeat is "defeat," and love is "love." We heap problems upon ourselves by calling trouble "misinterpretations," defeat "reconsideration," and love "companionship." Accurate communication depends upon correct descriptions.

What do we say to a hippopotamus? We say, "Hello, Hippopotamus!"—especially when it is our hippopotamus.

❦   ❦   ❦

No longer a boy, he was now fully a man and lines were beginning to crack his face and the youthful haircut could not conceal the oncoming gray. He was talking with his father about earlier days and, while every effort was made to avoid old conflicts, the young man finally said, "The thing I hated most about my growing up with you was your constant harping on 'my responsibility.'"

The parent acknowledged that that was often the matrix around which their father-son conversations turned, and, because neither had a desire to renew old and futile arguments, the discussion drifted to different topics. Yet the father wondered, "How could it be otherwise? How could a parent avoid a concern over a child's acceptance, or rejection, of responsibility?" How, indeed!

"Responsibility" may be a "parent word" filled with all the heavy, boring and exhausting tasks of human relationships. It may be used too often, too harshly and too accusingly, but it is a key concept without which the most primary bonds fail. "Responsibility" is a sign noting that a child has become a participating member of the community, it is a public notice that he has a place in the scheme of things, and that others go about their tasks with the assurance that he will go about his. Acceptance of responsibility is our personal contract with the universe.

We, as child and adult, may rebel at "responsibility," but tattered and torn, debased and ignored, this single word remains a judge of our past and a light for our future.

❧   ❧   ❧

There are few parents who, given the right situation and exhaustion, have not said to their children, "Don't do as I do, do as I say." The statement is usually followed by reflection on the part of parents and children alike, and parents usually feel guilty. Certainly there are reasons for the guilt, as society has generally condemned these words as both irresponsible and hypocritical.

But maybe society is wrong. There are enough authentic items about which one might feel guilty without denouncing those who, in either fits of anger or moments of honest introspection, say: "Don't do as I do, do as I say!" Such a proclamation may not be as hypocritical as we have been led to believe. Upon closer examination we may find the words to be more of a desire than a deceit.

Is it so wrong to expect our children, or society's children, to be better than we? Where is the error in urging the coming generations to behave more ethically than we have behaved? There is adequate reason for us to feel guilty regarding our actions, but why should we feel guilty for expressing our hopes? Upon examination we may find that society's future is more dependent upon the present day's teachings than upon its actions.

"Don't do as I do, do as I say," can be a statement of hypocritical arrogance; it also can be a prayer.

❧   ❧   ❧

There was a time when children were told that they shouldn't ask certain questions because the questions were either difficult or embarrassing. It still happens. These times arise because there are many questions which we would like to avoid as they put us "on the spot." A typical, if unfair, way of handling such questions is to suggest that the questioner was wrong for asking. It's an old trick: If you can't or won't answer the questions, suggest that the questioner is offensive.

The truth, however, is that "there are no bad questions, only bad answers." This insight of Isaac Bashevis Singer is true to the point of discomfort. We would like to avoid such wisdom because it is less risky to argue the validity of the question than to chance a wrong or stupid answer.

Yet these questions will not go away. The question has real value—the fact that it is not easily answered proves that—and items of value have staying power. Those questions which we so skillfully avoid do not disappear. Those penetrating questions which awaken us in the middle of the night are some of our best questions, and they deserve more than a suggestion that they are the product of momentary indigestion. Questions are truth at the dawn of creation, and they enjoy the tenacity of creation itself.

It would be well for us to nurture our questions for they are of intrinsic value. In time, and if we are fortunate, we may discover a few answers which are almost as good as our questions.

❧   ❧   ❧

A child was struck by a car. She died the next day.

The mind hears these facts, but it is loath to accept them. In a desperate move we ask that the sources be double checked, we shake our heads hoping that we are asleep and dreaming, we search for some cause or at least some one to blame. But, finally, the mind accepts the truth, and we know that there is no readily acceptable cause or obvious guilt.

How can we handle this tragedy? What words can relieve the pain?

There is very little relief, and we are aware that the passage of years will never reduce the mounting scar tissue. Still we might recognize that a child's life, even one cut short by an absurdity of existence, is full and rich. Here, as in so much of life, we do nothing but destroy ourselves by reading our sorrow into another's situation.

It sometimes seems that children are better equipped than adults to accept death. Perhaps in earlier times, when the death of children was more common, nature taught the child to live days fully and not to postpone happiness. The child is more concerned with living each day than what he or she would miss through sudden death. The child knows a secret we all should learn: the only way you can outpoint death is to pack every day with life.

To us, the death of a child is tragic and insane, but we

can know that the child did not waste his or her life. It would be less than an honorable memorial to the dead if we should waste ours.

❦   ❦   ❦

Parents do not rear children; they rear adults. It is a simple fact often ignored. All too often parents are concerned with what kind of children they have rather than by what kind of adults their children will become. The fact that Bobby may be a brat is not nearly as important as what kind of adult Robert will be. Peggy may be a shy child, but this fades into insignificance when we attempt to understand what kind of adult Margaret is in the process of becoming.

The child will be a child for only a few years. Whether the child is a little angel or a little devil is a question soon irrelevant. History is filled with children who were the apples of their parents' eyes who went on to become terrible adults; it is also filled with incorrigible children who grew up to be saints and statesmen. Whatever else might be said about these people, the one constant is that they were adults far longer than they were children, and it is the adults which history remembers. The child soon passes; the adult stays and stays.

Parents worry about children's behavior, as well they might. But a more significant worry is the behavior of the adults which their children are becoming. "Such a nice boy," and, "Such a nice girl," are compliments which always make parents proud, but this is the kind of pride "which goeth before destruction." The rearing of children is such a rapidly changing effort that every parent needs to make circumspection a major commitment.

The pleasant child is a joy to the family, but the pleasant adult is a blessing to the world.

❦   ❦   ❦

She must have been about four years old and stood well within the security of her own front yard. She stood there in innocence and did a very innocent thing: she waved at the passing cars.

It was a single act of friendliness along a very unfriendly road. The cars sped by, as is the way with cars and busy people, and it is doubtful that many acknowledged her cordial gesture. While it is quite possible that many would have liked to have acknowledged her, our surprise, slow responses and fast moving cars put her beyond our view before we could manage so much as a smile. No doubt many wondered what the little girl thought of these somber-faced drivers who ignored her waving hand.

The little girl is a symbol of our lives. There are many of us, perhaps most of us, who will spend much of our lives waving to the passing crowd of strangers who seem to neither recognize our gesture nor share our attempt at friendliness. They will pass by, and our efforts will seem foolish and unwanted.

Yet before we go into our house and shut the door against the uncaring traffic, both we and the little girl may learn an ancient lesson. It is not the acknowledgment or appreciation which makes the friendly gesture worthwhile. The reward is in the act itself. Those who bring humanness and gentleness into the world will rarely receive honors and acclaim. These people learned long ago that the great reward was the friends they had made, and all else is unnecessary.

Our rewards, also, could begin with a simple wave of our hand.

❦ ❦ ❦

If, by some trick of time, we could enter an earlier decade and meet ourselves as the children we were, what would we say? What kind of advice would we offer? What dangers would we describe?

Hardly a day goes by when we don't give serious consideration to the younger generations of which we were a part. How often we reflect on the words, "If I could do it over again..." or, "If I were younger..." or, "If I had known..."

We cannot live in the past, and we know it. We cannot live our lives again, and there is that within each of us which doesn't want to. But all these years, all this wisdom, and all these experiences should be of use.

And, of course, they are. The child we were still lives. In a very real way, we are the same person we always were. There have been changes, but the real issues and problems remain. What should we do with all the wisdom and advice that naturally emerges from our great experience? We could offer it to that child in our self with whom we are so well acquainted and of whom we are forgetful, and then we could sit back and be amazed at how wise we have become.

❦ ❦ ❦

The long-revered teaching, "Children should be seen and not heard," has pretty much passed from the child-rearing scene. Perhaps that's for the best. Children are far more than objects to be observed, admired or ignored by adults. They should have a place in the adult community which affirms their importance as participating human beings. Besides, they just may have something to say which will counter the easily accepted profundity of the more mature.

Our openness to their company, however, should not revoke the adult community's responsibility to teach the children to listen. Listening, not merely hearing, is a skill which cannot be learned at too young an age. It may be that we don't want to tell the child to "Shut up," but we do want to help the youngster to "Listen-up."

There is no pedagogical substitute for listening to adult conversation. The coming generations will be spoiled and provincial if they do not have the opportunity to experience the wisdom and foolishness of "grown-ups." Out of such exposure they will winnow their own wisdom or foolishness—as have we all.

❦   ❦   ❦

It's difficult to tell someone who has never had the experience what it is like to be a parent. We don't want to be cynical and list only the problems, nor do we want to be sentimental and recite only joys. We try to present a balanced view providing a fair share of both difficulties and thrills. If we are true to ourselves, it is likely that we will conclude by claiming that parenthood is one of the wonders and rewards of human life.

And so it is. We, however, should note that in the midst of the fun and fulfillment, along with the complexities and labors there is a goodly share of outright terror. There are sleepless nights, nagging fears, and the churning notion that tragedy is just beyond our sight. It may be that we will be lucky enough to escape the tragedy and the terror has no basis in fact. But terrible things do happen, and our worst fears are possible realities.

Regardless of the terror, we, like our forebears behind us and our prodigy before us, still willingly praise parenthood. We know the threatening Furies, but love makes the suffering tolerable. We will work on the problems, labor to transform the difficulties into potentials, keep the fear under some control, live with the terror that inhabits our quiet moments, and weep until our tears run dry, because love finally enables us to be parents.

Parenthood is pain and terror and suffering, but most of all it is love. In the midst of all which hurts and in spite of the tears, the awareness that we have loved and have been loved is reward enough.

❦   ❦   ❦

She said she wouldn't go to the party. When asked why, the answer was long in coming. Finally, the reason: "Because they'll play 'Pin the Tail on the Donkey' and people will laugh at me."

Her concern was not taken lightly. One by one recollections arose. Reluctantly other comments: "I fell down and was terrified," "I walked into another room and was humiliated," "I was always afraid." For years we buried our feelings about the game; buried them so deeply that we willingly exposed our own children to the same game and the same chance of ridicule.

It is a cruel game, but we are not cruel. We offer the game in the spirit of fun, and somewhere along the way we have become accustomed to the concept that other people's mistakes are funny. We have also learned and promoted the idea that humiliation is acceptable if the risk is shared by all.

Here's the rub. While the risks may be equal, the effects are not. In the game, each child has an equal chance to be a fool, but the feeling of foolishness will not be equal. For some, it's a game fairly played; to others, it's an experience not soon forgotten.

Unfortunately, the game is not limited to children's parties, and it masquerades under various guises. We, who are well into adulthood, still create an environment for failure, laugh at the humiliated, and pretend that it's all fair play.

It requires considerable maturity not to exchange cruelty with peers or leave it as a bitter inheritance.

❧   ❧   ❧

"Your children are not your children," wrote Kahlil Gibran in *The Prophet.* What could that possibly mean in a society which often assesses achievement or failure as a result of parenthood alone?

It means, at least, that children are not the sole products of parents. The wisdom does not exist—and perhaps should not exist—which allows the fathers and mothers among us to mold our children into the images we desire. It is not our task to sculpt children's minds or values as if they were clay. We may, if we are strong enough and lucky enough, influence their development. Even this may or may not be beneficial depending upon our insights and wisdom. In all likelihood, our children will mature in their own way, accepting some of our lessons and rejecting others. They build their own lives for their own time. It is highly possible that we will find much of this maturation process upsetting, and even frightening, but there are other influences and needs acting upon our children's lives.

We rear our children as best we can. We endeavor to build a society which will complement our efforts, we hope their peers are admirable, and we labor for a human and competent educational system. But the children develop their own lives, and parents have no option but to live with that fact.

"Your children are not your children," wrote Gibran generations ago, and such insight is redeeming wisdom for the pride-filled or guilt-stricken parents of each new generation.

🐦   🐦   🐦

It seems a pity that the human body cannot proclaim its emotional illness or health by raising or lowering its temperature. Even a minor cold is reflected by an increase of one's temperature and, no matter how insignificant the illness, a fever will bring forth care and sympathy. But not so with an emotional upset. Here, more often than not, all but the most major difficulties are ignored.

Nowhere is this more true than in the lives of our children. Should a child develop a fever, all kinds of measures are taken to insure his comfort and improvement. No one would think of telling a child to "behave himself and get rid of the flu." We would consider it insane for a parent to punish a child because he had measles. To "run a fever" forces the parent to take actions which will improve the child's health.

What a blessing it would be if there were a "thermometer" to measure the emotional health of our children. We who rush to our children's assistance when they have a fever, might then also rush to our children's aid when they signal a lack of love, or wonder, or appreciation. If there were a way to alert us to a growing emotional difficulty, surely we would be better parents and better friends to our children.

But there is no "thermometer for the emotions," and we are left to gauge as best we can the emotional well-being of our children. Surely this is a condition as important as their physical well-being. Since there is no method for measuring our children's emotional needs, perhaps it would be wise for us to offer them a little extra love, a little extra care, and a little extra understanding, just in case.

❦   ❦   ❦

Finally, what can we give our children? A good education? A loving home? A notable inheritance? Surely these are all wonderful gifts, but if we have only one gift to give, what might that be?

Perhaps that one great gift is: "the good example." Other gifts, education, money, and even love are inconsequential beside this one great gift. The state may provide a finer education than we could possibly afford, our money may be unwanted or insufficient when available, our love may be ignored or unrecognized. But the good example remains.

Our children may ignore the educational opportunities, they may foolishly expend their inheritance, and they may sentimentalize our love, but the good example stays on in their minds. It may inspire or it may haunt, but it will not be denied. Our children may ignore the channels we clear for them, may be singularly unmoved by our sacrifices, and may not return our love, but the good example will not be ignored. What they saw us do—how we managed our lives so that the stranger might survive, or served in order that another might find peace—will hold steady in their memories long after we are gone.

We want to give to our children, and we do. We assist with their education, sacrifice for their inheritance, and support them with our love. Yet if we want them to have something which will fire their lives, renew them when they are exhausted, and remain a constant reminder of our hopes and their possibilities, we should give them a good example. It is the most we can do.

❦   ❦   ❦

We expect so much from our children. Our expectations lead us to convey an insensitivity which is a burden upon our offspring and unfair to ourselves. We adults are not cruel or unfeeling, but we often act as if we were by allowing our expectations to guide our actions.

We expect our children to be responsible, learned and significant individuals, and we work our, and their, fingers to the bone in efforts to meet these expectations. No one discounts the worthiness of our desires, but we may question the priority. Might not we and our children build a more satisfying and enduring society if our first expectation was their happiness?

We are so concerned that our children be responsible, mature and intelligent, we often overlook their happiness. But happiness may be the key to the successful life. Frequently we consider happiness to be an incidental side-effect, but what goal is more to be desired?

What a wonderful legacy it would be if we were to expect our children to be happy. It might be that once happiness was achieved other values such as responsibility, maturity and intelligence would follow.

🦋   🦋   🦋

It continues to be true that "If you're not at home somewhere, you're not at home anywhere." While recognizing the essentially wandering character of the human being, we need to understand the sense of settledness which allows men and women to rest and relax.

Surely there is validity in the claim that draws attention to the fact that such "at home-ness" leads to a provincialism and a narrowness which, in turn, produces much possessiveness and bigotry. To allow our need for stability, however, to become a reason for exclusiveness and stinginess is to profane the concepts of home and hometown.

Life is consistent in its demand that each of us carries a sense of personal history. It is not important that such a history be a recitation of noble lives and famous deeds. It is only important that we recognize our vital life source—no matter how humble or coarse this might have been. Our private histories are important, not necessarily as examples of character, but as portrayals of process.

Home is the meeting ground of the past with its lessons and memories, the present with its joys and problems, and the future with its promises and hopes. Home becomes the guiding star which reminds us of yesterday and points our way to tomorrow.

🦋   🦋   🦋

THE GRAIN OF YOUR OWN WOOD

IV

*The defeated know, as only they can
know, "the grain of their own wood."*

The concept of comfort seems mysterious, and there are few of us who are prepared to describe the art of comforting someone or believe that we are its particularly talented practitioners. We may speak of someone who has a comforting word or knows the right thing to do in demanding situations, but we hesitate when the duty is ours, and we are the comforters. It would seem that others hold some magic touch or have perfected some difficult skill.

Comforting, however, simply calls for caring people who will stand alongside. That is all there is to it. Thus understood, comfort is not a complicated performance. We need no special skills or divine gifts. We are requested to break the loneliness, the emptiness and the starkness of loss and fear. To be needed is all that is necessary. We are not miracle workers who can bring back that which is gone, scarcely any of us have the skills or gifts of healing which can relieve pain or change the course of disease, and there are few solutions to the most severe problems in life.

All this the one who needs comfort already knows. We are not asked to be that which we cannot be; those in pain know our limitations at least as well as we do. What is requested, and what is needed, is one who will stand solidly by the stricken. Most of us can confront almost any tragedy as long as we do not have to confront it alone.

To comfort, to stand alongside, is a restoring task. It is a task each of us can perform.

❧ ❧ ❧

After pain and suffering have done their work, when grief and sorrow have completed their tasks, and although labor and study lie in ashes, there remains the eternal potential.

There is always the potential of undiscovered avenues of vitality which no pain, sorrow or disappointment can destroy. The potential of new life can only be denied by those who consciously refuse to recognize it, for its objective reality is omnipresent.

This is the essential reason why both religion and society have consistently condemned the legitimization of suicide. Suicide is an act against the potential of new achievement, and neither state nor temple can tolerate such an attack upon the future. The essence of human development is inextricably bound to the potential of a richer, more satisfying and less sorrowful tomorrow.

An act of suicide only superficially says, "I am through with life." Its more authentic message is, "Life is through with me: it has no more to offer me." Against this message one hears the counterclaim: "The potentials of life are inexhaustible. The potential of tapping new streams of significance is ever- present, even in the depths of pain or sorrow."

And who are we, we frail and myopic creatures, to assume that the potentials of new insights and new achievements are not ours to grasp, or that tomorrow does not harbor a surprise?

❦　❦　❦

"All good things must come to an end." We learned this at someone's knee, but memory is inadequate to recall either teacher or time. The lesson, however, remains. Hardly a day goes by—and never a week—when the wisdom doesn't come rushing, usually uninvited, into our consciousness.

Good things do come to an end. There is no escaping that elementary truth. Still, neither the simplicity nor the truth of the phrase makes for its easy acceptance. We would never confess our doubts to our sophisticated friends, but in the quiet of our individual lives we clench our fists, fight back tears, and say, "Why?"

In these moments we reflect upon a personal secret. We mutter to ourselves that maybe what or whom we miss hasn't come to an end. And maybe it hasn't. Little proof may be available to substantiate our wishes, but it's no great crime to believe that the good may not be finished.

In truth, good things do have a way of returning, and who are we to predict tomorrow? What omniscient power gives us permission to judge the future? It may be that the best way for dealing with the universal wisdom which teaches, "All good things must come to an end," is to nod our heads and say, "Probably so," and then to whisper to ourselves, "Perhaps not."

❦   ❦   ❦

Only the color of her hair revealed her age. Certainly, there wasn't the slightest evidence of any loss of the quick mind or the sharp tongue when she told the audience: "Growing old is not for sissies."

As usual, she was correct. Some of life's most hurtful acts come at this time: the loss of a spouse, failing powers, forfeiture of identity which often comes with retirement, slippage of mental and physical capacities, and an inability to maintain health are only a few of the calamities.

So what should we do? Perhaps we should throw ourselves on the mercy of those who are younger and seek perpetual care. Perhaps we should ignore reality and claim that such a fate cannot and will not happen to us. Or perhaps we should spend our days whimpering about the unfairness of life or become lost in nostalgia. Or we could say to ourselves that old age is a part of life, just like every other part, with good times and bad, and if the bad out-mans the good we will do our best and live with it.

Old age may be the greatest time of life for some, but for most it will carry more than its share of miseries. Rather than bemoaning our fate, we might recognize that life's great problems come only after the years of living when we are better prepared. We couldn't have handled these diffi-culties when we were young. We weren't strong enough, stubborn enough, or smart enough. We get the true chal-lenges in our advanced years when we're tough. It's not a time for sissies.

❧   ❧   ❧

It was the twilight of a long day, and the room, always sunless, was now almost dark. During the hours of discus-sion, they had become shadows who responded to each other in patterns grown familiar over the years. There was a hard decision to be made, and the many words had gradually worn away the topic until only the nub re-mained.

"It seems to me," he said with a voice grown weary through experience, "that every person must try something beyond normal capabilities in order to know the grain of one's own wood."

Here, finally, was the issue: to attempt a task which can't be done.

This was not a "heavy responsibility" which would de-mand much and offer little. This was not a "challenge" which through Herculean efforts might earn one the hon-ors of labor and public acclaim. This was not a warning of failure which would tempt old fears and induce sleepless nights. This was an invitation to be defeated.

Defeat, unlike failure, which can be modified by excuses, hammers at its victim until he or she slumps with exhaustion. Defeat, like a malignancy gone wild, moves through the being affecting every vessel, every nerve ending, every emotion.

The defeated know, as only they can know, "the grain of their own wood." The ancients had other words: some called it "the fear of the Lord;" others, "the beginning of wisdom."

ồ   ồ   ồ

When faced with suffering and tragedy, most of us long for a miracle. We do this in spite of the fact that our minds tell us that miracles would rain havoc upon our planet. If miracles did abound, accomplishments would be washed away by a flood of chance. Kindness and generosity would be ignored as we sought to appease that which could ease our suffering or grant our desire by a single, supernatural act. A miracle, in truth, is a frightening thing and is more sensibly dreaded than desired.

Isn't mercy what we really want in a time of difficulty and sorrow? Mercy is the affirmation that the process which reduced pain before will reduce it again, and the understanding that those whom we have helped will now come to our aid. Mercy is the awareness that no one has surrendered and all which can be done is being done. Mercy is the support and love which is desperately needed in lonely hours.

Miracles have a strange and other-worldly quality about them, but mercy belongs to us. We humans, who have feet of clay and often stumble, are the conduits of mercy. It is to us that the pleas for mercy are directed. Mercy is our work.

When all our hopes have been dashed against the wall of reality, we may cry out for a miracle, but we should expect mercy. In fact, the two have much in common. From a distance, mercy often looks like a miracle and, perhaps, that is miracle enough.

❦   ❦   ❦

We are often told to "take the long view." That advice is not to be dismissed as there is significant need to put our immediate causes and cares into perspective. The difficulties of our days seem to shrink when they are placed within the context of our larger lives and possibilities.

But there are other times when the "long view" is impossible and only the immediate situation is appropriate. We have experiences when the future is so complex and so threatening that only careful attention to the present will do. Each of us has had personal contact with those developments in life which foreclose on the future, and any attempt to project our thoughts beyond the next hour or day is folly.

We must live each day with the full understanding that tomorrow's needs will be met with whatever resources tomorrow finds available. In this context, the phrase, "I live day by day," is not an expression of irresponsibility or pessimism, it is the only valid approach to the present pain, and the single hope for a better future. When life seems to be falling apart and tomorrow is a spinning abstraction, we work with the only item which is real—the present.

There are moments when the next five minutes is all the future we can, or should, accept.

When the past is barren and the future bleak, we discover a marvelous gift: today. For it, we have all the resources we can use, and find all the rewards we need.

There comes a time in the process of grieving when the sense of loss is lessened. At that moment, we are tempted to feel guilty. That is a mistake. We have simply become participants in the more practical aspects of immortality.

At such a juncture the eternal quality of our lives has been reemphasized. We are experiencing the elements in life which are untouched by death.

We are not making an excursion into the otherworldly, but recognizing a common product of intense human interaction. Death is only a partial separation. For good or evil, there is some part of each of us which is immortal. We will live after we die within our spouses, our children, our companions, and even our enemies. They, also, will live within us. It is folly to claim that death ends it all. For some death is a mighty loss, for others it is but a pause, but for no one is it an ending or a forgetting. We are all immortal.

Immortality is not something strange and supernatural. It is part and parcel of mortality—an extension of our participation in life. Each day we are confronted by, and we are part of, everlasting life. We are all participants and partners in an immortal experience.

There is a fifth season of the year when winter is gone and spring has not quite arrived. It is a natural season because the movement from winter to spring is never easy, and winter does not surrender with pleasant grace. Winter holds on, attacking when we are least expectant and exposing our newfound hopes for spring. In these moments we need to recognize the enduring word of the calendar and know that the cold season may try again, but it cannot reverse the oncoming spring.

There also is a fifth season in our lives. The new life after the long winter can be discouraged by the late season storms, but our newfound life will only be delayed and not destroyed. There may be weakness, but not the same disease; there may be depression, but not the same grief; there may be a continuing sense of loss, but not the brooding sense of despair. It is important to understand that in spite of setbacks, the winter of our life is over. Brief storms only mark the changing season, not the return of winter.

The fifth season is noted by the scar tissues which bother us and the "blues" which come as uninvited guests, but their claims are limited. There remains the inescapable logic that winter has come to its end. With a firm understanding of that truth before us, we will realize that only springtime awaits.

❦   ❦   ❦

No one wants to fail, but failure may be the most persistent teacher any of us will know. When victories are reduced to excursions in nostalgia, and defeats have been rendered irrelevant by the benevolence of excuses, failure remains to challenge, to instruct, and to probe.

Failure remains because it is an inside thing. Our failures have a way of staying with us. They do not desert in good times or in bad. They cannot be drowned by the shouts of victories or lost in a crowd of alibis. They quietly and constantly remain a part of us.

These failures remain either to destroy or instruct. They can destroy if we deny them and thereby deny ourselves, if we allow a loss of confidence and courage, or if we use past failures as excuses to deny future possibilities. Or, failure can instruct by giving new perspectives to our lives, and by providing insights into our strengths and weaknesses. It can teach us that humility is quality won through experience, and that arrogance betrays immaturity.

Failure, as a teacher which knows few equals, can tutor us in the art of acceptance as we learn there are some things we should not, need not, and cannot do. Failure is the genesis of wisdom.

❧   ❧   ❧

One of life's most challenging tasks is to revise dreams. We all have dreams. We have given birth to dreams and labored to make them realities. We abandon dreams only when we are exhausted and hope is broken. We destroy our dreams only when they prove impossible and always with an abiding sadness. To revise dreams, however, requires other talents.

Dull, indeed, are those who live without dreams. Still more unfortunate may be those who cling to their dreams in the face of certain failure. Between these two, the lost and the hopeless, we find those who practice the ancient and continuing art of revising. They rework, rekindle, and reassemble their dream to make it fit the new demands and the new age. These do not despair, and they do not abandon. They have chosen a more difficult process.

It takes no special skill to pretend that we traffic in reality and have no truck with dreams and dreamers. The pedestrian ways of our lives will be adequate witness to such a claim. It requires no unusual talent to give up and, sighing, note that such was not the right dream nor the right time. The loss of spring in our steps will confess our decision. But to examine and reconfigure the dream, to breathe new life into battered parts, to mend tears and to build anew, is to believe in the dream and keep it vital. Our dream is marred, but our care, our awareness and our revising enables it to be a continuing resurrection in and for our lives.

❦   ❦   ❦

In the world of emotions and feelings there are actions and reactions as necessary as those found in the rational world. The many emotions react to one another to protect the mind and body from destruction.

Such a situation arises in the human condition when grief results from loss and prevents the ascent of panic. Grief is a feared emotion, and this fear often prohibits our understanding of its vital contribution to our lives. It makes the immediate fact of loss tolerable. Grief fills the mind with its own all-encompassing presence and retards the possibility of chaos.

Grief gives us "something to do" and thus protects us from being panicked and paralyzed by the emptiness and the loneliness. At the moment of loss and sorrow, we desperately need time to reassemble the broken pieces of our lives, and a diversion which can deflect the many threats

which compete for our attention. Grief always arrives uninvited and unwanted; a tattered guest we had hoped to
evade. But it performs its sad duties and holds us together
until the first rays of the new day begin to appear. Knowing its place, it then leaves, and we emerge from its presence enabled to do what could not have been done without
its necessary contributions.

Grief enters our lives as a threat, and leaves as a healer.

❦   ❦   ❦

One of the amazing things about human beings is their
ability to rebound. In spite of defeats, disappointments and
heartbreaks, we bounce back to face the new day. Often
we wonder just how many more times we will be able to
gather the pieces and continue, but we do it again and
again. After the night's sleep, the new day finds us back
working on what seemed impossible a few hours earlier.

Why? What is it that forces us back into the fray? Why
don't we just give up? After all, who will truly miss this effort, and what difference will it make?

But we don't give up. We keep coming back even when
the rewards are minimal and the labor exhausting. We
come back because there remains the continuing possibility that this time we might succeed, and success has its
own reward. To rebound is to try again, and to prove to
ourselves anew that the task is not greater than we are. No
one, finally, can pay us for this. It is an inner push, a sense
of self-esteem, and the unwillingness to quit, which moti-
vate.

When self-esteem seems to be breaking, a quick word
from a friend urges the extra attempt, and the will returns.
As we grow older some of the buoyancy wanes, but the de-

sire to rebound does not fade, and therein lies the hope for us all.

❦   ❦   ❦

Men and women have been described as "deciding animals." Other creatures which roam this earth do so either by instinct or, in the few cases of highly developed intelligence, by making rare and simple choices. But the human race decides, and this marks us as unique.

It therefore may be that living becomes most difficult when we are confronted by indecision. We have learned to live with misfortune and mistakes, but we seldom learn to tolerate the unknown or the indecisive. For many of us, the fact of adversity is less difficult to accept than the possibility of adversity. We can endure all kinds of reverses as long as we know what they are, but the emptiness of not knowing is intolerable.

Yet we will not be exempt from the moments, and sometimes months, of uncertainty. The times when "it may be this or it may be that" have been and will continue to be a part of our lives. No one escapes the bleakness of neither knowing what has happened nor what to do.

The lesson here is simple and direct: wisdom lies not only in the correct thought and deed, but also in understanding that there are times when neither our thoughts nor our deeds prevail. In these times of powerlessness someone or something will make the decision. Then, at that decisive moment which is not ours, we are challenged to make a crucial decision: what to do next.

It sometimes seems that many of us are intellectually and emotionally equipped to handle the great problems of society and life, but are singularly ill-equipped to handle the day-to-day situations which wear down our abilities and resources. We like to think that we would know what to do if some catastrophe struck and our sacrifice was needed; it is the struggle with the everyday problems—the difficulty with children, the subtle antagonism between spouses or the nagging illness which fails to gain sympathy from either friends or physician—which gnaws at our senses of stability and worth.

Still, our ability to withstand the everyday pressures is the mark of both personal strength and true greatness. Worthy challenges rarely demand the noble and public sacrifice. Greatness is an immediate quality and is exhibited by those who have confronted the unheralded and boring daily tasks while maintaining their personal integrity and sense of humor. Unfortunately, we often do a better job of preparing our children to struggle bravely for some lofty goal than to survive the day in, day out routine of ordinary employment.

One hopes that there will come a time when forty years at the same job deserves more than a gold watch, and thirty years of rearing children is cause enough for a hero's reward. It may be that we have been giving the ticker tape parades and keys of the city to the wrong people.

❦   ❦   ❦

Anyone can be happy when the future is full of promise, and life seems ready to grant every wish. To be happy when the future is rosy requires no talent. Genius is required when the days ahead appear bleak. Difficult days have been a substantial part of the past, and there is no reason to assume that the future will be exempt. Time goes on, and so do we.

That's the good news: we go on. This on-goingness is one of our better traits. Recognizing that we can't change the future by fearing it, we go about our everyday business. This act of not stopping, of accepting the world warts and all, is strength personified. It is life affirming itself in the face of inevitability. Doing what must be done is more than passive acquiescence; it is an affirmation of strength and character.

To do what needs to be done when it no longer has to be done is the challenge which awaits all. Excuses are ever at hand when times are tough, but our self-esteem and sense of life demand more than excuses. There is a peculiar healing in continuing the process of living; of starting that which will never be finished.

If the future isn't rosy, then we will do what is required of us. If this isn't happiness, it must be the next best thing.

❦   ❦   ❦

There are times in life when the only thing any of us can do is to soften reality. We would wish that time could be reversed, that someone had acted sooner or better, or that some miraculous healing balm were ours to dispense. Alas, these are desires which stark reality rarely allows.

There are times in all lives when those who have always been able to "do something" find that their abilities no longer apply. Those associated with action and effort find themselves useless in the areas where no act will aid. In this helpless time, special talents prevail. In this time of acute pain, the strong hand and the caring word may be the greatest gifts of all.

The words, "I wish I could do more," are constantly uttered by those who feel they are not doing enough. What they fail to realize is that they are doing precisely what is needed when they are assisting in making the intolerable situation tolerable. One need not feel guilty for not doing more in an environment where more cannot be done. To offer a strong hand in friendship, an honest revelation of caring love, and the willingness to join in a silent walk with another along a lonely and sorrowful path is exactly the right and proper thing to do.

"Outrageous fortune" is a part of human life. We are protected most of the time, but no one escapes forever. Then, when all life seems to dissolve, there is a desperate need for those whose single and worthy talent can soften reality. Blessed are these, the ones who are there—simply there.

ಌ   ಌ   ಌ

Ridiculous as it seems, there is a benevolence in common agony. If we could simply recognize that all are caught up in the absurdities of existence, and that no reward is great enough to right these wrongs, we might be a little kinder to each other, and the human community might not be such an impossible goal. Why should we, who suffer and have suffered, be heartless toward our fellow human beings who too have suffered?

Not that the old answers have been tried and found wanting. There is much wisdom born in the sufferings of past ages.

Job's great affirmation: "Naked I came from my

mother's womb, and naked I return; the Lord gave, and the Lord has taken away; blessed be the name of the Lord," still rings true, even in a society which cannot remember Job. This message to our time is not so much one of divine omniscience as it is of the inescapable reality that a full life demands not only the enjoyment of what is given, but the surrender of what is taken.

The total understanding of existence requires an awareness that everything is "on loan." The moment we begin to think in terms of permanence we place ourselves in immediate candidacy for great sorrow. Because of the remaining darkness which surrounds each life, we learn, sooner or later, to both accept what life gives and to part with everything. This, of course, is a pretty good working definition of maturity.

❦   ❦   ❦

There are no shortages of shadows in our lives. When death takes one we love, a shadow falls across our lives; when illness so affects our being that our days are marked with pain, a darkness covers all hopes; when our career lies shattered at our feet, our plans, no matter how carefully considered, are eclipsed; when our children are harmed or harm themselves, each night initiates new terrors; when knowledge is used for folly and intelligence is captured by evil, gloom seems everywhere; when love leaves and our offers go unaccepted, clouds of despair claim their dominion.

If, in our realism, we no longer expect miracles, then let us be done with them. When we can no longer look for the miraculous, let us, with quickened objectivity, look for surprises. In the darkness of our lives we, if we are willing, can see that which was not available to us in the light. The shadow, by whatever name, which darkens our living is the same shadow which provides an opportunity to see what the dimness reveals.

Like the eclipse of the sun which surprises us with a sight of the brightest stars, so the eclipse of our joys can amaze us with displays which, if unequal to the bright happiness, can impress with a different kind of brilliance. No one escapes the shadows which crowd our globe, but even here, perhaps especially here, one may hear a quiet voice whisper, "Look and stand ready to be surprised."

❧   ❧   ❧

Problems are not only stumbling blocks in our lives, they also are milestones marking our continuing development. The events which came our way and seemed to bar our progress have often proved to be the challenges which stimulated mind and life to new, and undreamed of, heights.

Others have noted that we should pity those who have never had problems too big for them. People who have lived their days without the pressures of conflicting demands, the difficulties born of ambition and need, and the pain that comes from failure, are usually shallow and childish souls unfit for the world's honors or promises. These men and women surely develop false views of life as they move from one simple solution to another. How they must lack the insight which comes only from the caustic knowledge of defeat, and how they must bore their companions.

Few of us want problems, but how limited we would be without them. Even fewer of us would eagerly taste the bitter fruit of defeat, but without the losses how could we recognize the joy of victory? We would surely seek escape from tragedy for its pain is too much for us, yet we can emerge from the most heartbreaking experience with a new grasp of the wonder and love of life.

Every problem has hidden deep within it a rewarding potential. To recognize and use this truth is to make existence worthwhile and give every tomorrow the rich gift of today.

❦   ❦   ❦

YES, YOU CAN

V

We've been afraid before, we've been lost

before, and we've been sure that life

was too difficult before. Yet here we are,

a bit battlescarred to be sure,

but we got through.

"She'll never amount to anything" was the common remark. Certainly, the odds were not in her favor. She was born in poverty, reared in the most unstable environments, and was educated in the poorest schools. She was neglected: undernourished, undertrained and unappreciated.

Yet she did amount to "something." Indeed, she excelled at those exact points where others had failed her. Not knowing the love and support of a mother, she became a mother which others would envy. Denied the educational opportunities others took for granted, she provided increased opportunities for all. Having been reared in bleak slums, she shared the qualities of acquired beauty.

Why? What mysterious psychological, sociological or biological agents brought success where failure should have been?

No one knows. Nor are we likely to learn. Perhaps it was some chance encounter with one of those rare souls who enlightens and inspires. Perhaps some residual and reticent gene asserted itself. Perhaps some event of personal or social significance forced a subtle change of attitude which opened new vistas. A final and complete answer is impossible.

But the essential fact is that her life was not limited by the quality of existence. For reasons we may never know and she may never understand, she refused to accept the confines of environment. Thus her history is another in the long list of eternal examples proving that life is not necessarily crushed by adversity.

Most of us were reared with the maxim: "Nothing ventured, nothing gained." The wisdom of this expression was born of the people who recognized the energy and promise of this land. They also knew that the land, its resources, and its people were not passive contributors to the available enterprises, but were reluctant to part with their gifts unless others were willing and able to share their fortunes and talents. "If you want something, venture something," was the common creed, and it was equally understood that if you didn't venture you would not achieve.

The old maxim, however, may be lost in our new age. There seems to be a trend, which percolates down to each of us, to protect what we have and raise walls against the new day. Our present maxim seems to be, "Nothing ventured, nothing lost." This new schooling holds that we must keep what we have, garner and hoard our resources, and, in general, husband our assets against the claims of the future.

But if we have become a people who are afraid to try the new lest we lose something of the old, we have become a dull and vacant generation. If we have become so protective of our little portions that we refuse to take risks, we have become a weak reflection of our forebears and a disappointment to our children.

"Nothing ventured, nothing lost" is a cheap imitation of the wisdom, "Nothing ventured, nothing gained." We will have failed parents and fettered posterity if fear of loss limits our field of vision. We give witness to life's vitality when we affirm that yesterday is the proper stake for tomorrow.

From time to time each of us is faced with a personal situation which seems impossible. The dimensions of the problem exhaust the mind and cripple the will. "I don't believe I can handle this," is our steady fear, and we stand on the edge of surrender.

When these occasions arise, we need someone who will say to us, "Yes, you can." This statement is not a sentimental comment or one which is bereft of realism. It is not false optimism or a childish whistling in the dark. "Yes, you can," is the encouragement which we need. It's a positive suggestion which mobilizes the forces of our individual lives in order that we might meet the coming crisis.

The often unacknowledged fact of our lives is that we have met problems before and have survived. Surely this new difficulty carries a variety of unknowns, but the old difficulties were equipped with their surprises also. We've been afraid before, we've been lost before, and we've been sure that life was too difficult before. Yet here we are, a bit battlescarred to be sure, but we go through.

There are moments, however, when no one is there to urge us on. When this is our lot, it is necessary to sit down in a quiet place, bring our minds to a rest, and await the private voice of our gathered history which eventually and inevitably says, "Yes, you can." We cannot believe this actually happens, we cannot believe that the still voice speaks, but the experience of the ages says "Yes, you can."

❧   ❧   ❧

A vacation is not determined by where we go, what we see, whom we visit, or how long we stay. A vacation is determined by what we pack.

The beach can sparkle and the sea beckon, but if work

tumbles out of our suitcases we might as well have stayed home. The mountains can offer unmatched panoramas, but if difficulties claim our attention, the vistas fall on unseeing eyes. Friends may offer cheer and kin rekindle joys long forgotten, but if our problems have been packed as carefully as our pajamas, the good times will not roll. We may extend our vacations through weeks and months, we may sail the oceans and fly over continents, but if troubles are tucked into the corners of our trunks, our days are simply routine.

A vacation is not simply going somewhere; it is a state of being. The hours of planning, the labor in preparation, or the costs don't matter. If we cannot separate ourselves from the fears, the worries, and the issues which plague our ordinary days, we might be honest enough with ourselves to know that we will not take a vacation.

Before we leave on the next vacation, we should pack our troubles in our most worn suitcase, take that bag to the attic and leave it. Once that's done, where we go, what we see, whom we visit, or how long we stay are all irrelevant—the vacation has already begun.

❦   ❦   ❦

Edison's famous remark, "Genius is one percent inspiration and ninety-nine percent perspiration," still rings true. Hard work—often dull, monotonous complicated work—remains necessary.

It is common in our time to refer to others as having the ability to perform well but lacking the willingness to do so. Innumerable parents have been told that their children are certainly smart enough but that they do not "apply themselves." This is somewhat easier to take than the accusation that the children are dull. We would rather be lazy than stupid and, surely, we hold the same wish for our children.

But what difference does it make? If we, our children, our friends, and our leaders have the potential but do not make the effort, aren't the results the same? Is the person who lacks a willingness to labor more valuable than one who has limited intellectual capacity? If we do not perform necessary tasks because we won't, rather than we can't, what difference does it make, and who cares how smart we are?

We recognize that potential is promising, but results are indispensable. Society is more likely to profit from practical providers than phantom millionaires.

ಶ   ಶ   ಶ

Computers, magnificent as they are, are limited by human input. If the information read into the computer is incorrect, the data released is incorrect. This has given rise to the computer age aphorism: "Garbage in, garbage out."

Here, as in so many places, this newfound understanding has application in our daily, non-electronic lives. We are bound by the limits of the accuracy and nature of incoming data. If the received information is true and generous, the released analysis will be true and generous; if the received communication is false and self-serving, the product of our discernment will be false and self-serving. "Garbage in, garbage out."

With such knowledge we might influence our emotional well-being with new understanding and control. If our days are dull and emptiness permeates our lives, we might examine the "programs" we have entered into our most personal computers. If we have accepted only dullness and emptiness, what can we expect? A little self-discipline which requires that the good news be balanced with the bad, that promises accompany problems, and that insight be joined with mistakes, will do much to improve the emotional quality of our lives. If "Garbage in, garbage out" is true, its opposite will be equally true: "Excellence in, excellence out." We may not be able to control all input, but what we can control will determine whether the output is trash or treasure.

❦   ❦   ❦

Much good might come from a public relations push on behalf of creative lowered expectations. This simply means that rather than always reaching for the moon, we might try reaching for the next room. It is better to have little, and seemingly insignificant successes, than no successes at all. Those little successes maintain our sense of self-worth and provide us the courage to seek the next possibility. To move from the impossible dream to the possible reality is the result of creative lowered expectation, and while such action will not gain headlines, it will gain improvements.

Improvement is the goal. There are few breakthroughs in this life. Most of us will gain goals and sustain self-respect with the steady improvements in day-to-day living. Indeed, improvement is a key to happiness; perfection is a door to melancholy.

It has been said that people who seek to lose fifty pounds of excess weight can be divided into two categories: those who try to lose the weight in two months and fail, and those who try to lose the weight, one pound a week for a year, and succeed. So it is with most of life: we can seek perfection and fail, or we can seek improvement and suc-

ceed. The present question for us is not, "What wonderful
thing will we do tomorrow?" but "How much improved is
today over yesterday?"

The ancient call, "Be ye perfect" is a theological appeal.
The less exciting charge, "Be ye improved," is a survival
technique.

❦   ❦   ❦

It was a bright, warm and sunshine-filled day. These simple facts were beyond doubt. There wasn't a cloud in the
sky, and the southern breeze encouraged open windows
and unbuttoned coats. We couldn't believe it was February.

February is always marked with cloudy skies and the reality or threat of snow. How could one account for these
blue skies and warm winds? Who could answer for this
comfort where only complaints had gone before? How does
one live with a blessing when a bane was expected? Who
pays when April appears in February?

No one pays. Balmy days in the midst of winter are
happy accidents. We who expect the constant parade of
bleak days are always surprised when a break in the
weather proves beneficial. We fail to realize that every
winter has its moments of springtime sky and thawing
breezes, and these are as natural as the raw wind and the
blizzard.

This, also, is true of our lives. No involvement is so
bleak, no situation so constantly desperate, that there isn't
a happy accident which rekindles the mind and lightens
each life. It requires no extra insight to find these moments; it requires an acquired blindness to ignore them.

There will always be April days in February. What a

pity it would be if we, in our efforts to escape the cold, should sit in our houses with shades drawn and miss them.

❧ ❧ ❧

Some day we should erect a monument to the plodders of all ages. They were the ones who seldom received the honors and the acclaim, but they did the work and made the improvements. They were the ones who realized that, after the parade and the speeches, the world would have changed little. All the tasks of life still waited. The plodders labored on their insignificant projects and they made the difficult advances.

Our problems will be solved, and our ills relieved, by the day in and day out plodding which we must do. If we want a better society, we work at it, we plod, and slowly we build a better society. If we want a better marriage, we work at it, we plod, and slowly our marriage improves. If we want better relationships with our children, we work at them, we plod, and slowly relationships mend. The plodders make improvements. The sprinters make dust.

Plodding is not a way to live. It is the way we live. It's all right if we don't accomplish every goal in our lives, and if we are not acclaimed by strangers. It's all right if the job's not finished, for there will always be tomorrow, and if we are not there, someone will be. It is only necessary that we learn the noble art of plodding. And when we do, we are in the company of saints.

❧ ❧ ❧

One of the thrills of life is to be a part of something which is great or becomes great. This is one of the reasons young people join causes others think are foolish, or older people return for reunions others think are folly. To be a part of a movement, or a moment, of noted history is reward enough regardless or what others think.

We often belittle ourselves by saying that we are no more than what we are. "What you see is what you get," is the popular expression. Our trafficking in ordinariness is a common attempt at humility, but one wonders if we really believe it—or should believe it.

Each of us is more than we seem. We are both burdened and uplifted by the events which have been part of our lives. The battles we fought for nation or cause, the books we've read, the people we have met, and the places which reside in our memories are all a part of us. We could no more reject them than we could reject kin or limb.

It is a mark of benevolent pride to remember an event of lasting importance, to walk the halls of a noble institution, or to see justice reign where only injustice lived before and say, I was a part of that!

❦   ❦   ❦

Life is not a "thing," but a "process," and each of us is part of that process. Just as we are constantly changing in the submicroscopic aspects of our being, so we are changing in our manners, thoughts and lifestyles. Even while we sleep, we move, for our dreams are steadily at work revising the way we think about ourselves and others. There is no escaping the process, not even by death itself.

And why should life be otherwise? Who could long stand the steady repetition of the static existence? These days which are engulfed in a steady flood of nostalgia should not tempt us to return to the "good old days." Only those whose memories are short, or who have no memories, would truly seek the re-establishment of any former age. We know, deeper than our excursions into nostalgia, that we cannot go back—and we wouldn't if we could.

Life exists on the growing edge. We need to travel light carrying those values which can act as sensors. Truth, love, beauty and justice float well on the stream of life and they serve us ably. Those who burden themselves with weighty prejudices and obligations of fashion are recognized by their struggles against change and their constant complaining. The processes of life demand that we carry our possessions loosely.

Life is going to change whether we like it or not. It may be that, if we slow down and listen, we will hear not only the sound of society at work and play, but also the music of the spheres. When we hear the music, we will want to dance.

❦   ❦   ❦

"Ask and you shall receive" is one of the better known Biblical passages. It is one of those teachings which extends a dual gift: one for our benefit and one for our ruin.

We tempt destruction when we ask and receive the wrong things. Like the spoiled rich child we find ourselves surrounded by what we wanted but gives us little satisfaction. We ask for gadgets and conveniences, we ask for immediate happiness, and we ask for satisfaction. And they are received. But the gadgets break or wear out, the conveniences become bores, happiness seems fleeting and our satisfactions grow, all too rapidly, into dissatisfactions. We could ask again, but what good would it do?

It might work well for us to ask for those things which

NOTES ON AN UNHURRIED JOURNEY   97

aren't so much in demand. We might ask for the wisdom that our petty desires not overwhelm. We might ask for courage in order that we may seek that which has lasting value and no longer feel a need to hide behind the facade of some cheap gratification. We might ask for a single friend who could both recognize our pain and laugh at our jokes.

We can ask with a sense of foolishness or profundity, but always a note of self-warning should accompany our request. Such a note would read: "Proceed with care—you may get what you ask for."

❧　❧　❧

The can-do people in our society may not be as special as we think. They have three characteristics which are by no means impossible for others to attain.

They are inner-directed. The can-do types do not wait for someone to suggest an idea or answer. They seek answers which are satisfactory to them. The questioning and the seeking rise from within, and they are not quieted until a solution is found.

They are self-reliant. The can-do men and women are not dependent upon others for stimulation, steady guidance, or justification. These are the ones who truly believe that they have the energy and strength, both physical and intellectual, to make the necessary choices and perform the required duties.

They are adventurous. The can-do folk are excited about the possibilities of life, about the quality of the future, and how they might be engaged in that which is new and different. Thus attempted, life can never be dull and each new search expands vistas and possibilities.

If these are special characteristics, they are special only because we make them so. We may elect to be a can-do society: a can-do people. The choice is ours. We, as millennia of saints and sages promised, can be as gods.

❦   ❦   ❦

Life, in spite of what many of us have been taught, is not a test. It is not something which we can fail. It simply is. Life has one purpose and one purpose only: to be lived. As Woody Allen wisely noted, "If you show up, you pass."

Some will argue that such an understanding of life will lead to rampant hedonism and gross irresponsibility. In response, we might suggest that the opposition's theory has produced its full share of hedonism and irresponsibility.

If we recognize that life is not a test, and that it is impossible to fail, we are   free to do what human beings should do best: survive and enjoy.

What a wonderful thing it would be if all entered into their worldly adventure with an awareness that survival is the only curriculum, that joy and care are the only assignments, and that there is no final exam. Graduation could then be a time without regrets, shame, or failures, when we all look back and say: "Wasn't that something!"

❦   ❦   ❦

The great English novelist, E. M. Forster, never owned more than he could pack in a single medium-size suitcase. The fact that he was an Oxford don living in his "rooms" helped, but still we feel a challenge. Could we do as well? Could we face the fact that we are more than what we own? Could we travel light?

Experienced travelers, whether seasoned in journeys of planet or mind, are free with their advice. "Be comfortable, neat, clean, and even adequately fashionable, but don't take more than is needed. Get it all into one suitcase, and remember, you must carry it. Wash when necessary and learn to 'make do' with as few changes as possible. Keep in mind that people are more interested in who you are than what you wear. Don't let the burdens of luggage keep you from enjoying what you are travelling to enjoy."

Do we listen? Or, when it finally comes time to pack, do we find ourselves taking more than necessary "just in case"? We don't need to burden ourselves. It isn't necessary to restrict the enjoyment of life because we have so much baggage. But it takes courage, organization and a sense of adventure to travel light. Perhaps it's a matter of trust. After all the years of toting these bags, do we dare trust life enough to practice travelling light?

❦   ❦   ❦

We often forget that an achievement is simply a dream upon which we have labored. The difference between dreams and achievements is, more often than not, our labor.

Accidents, unanticipated complications, and natural events may block the path which leads from dream to achievement, and tragedy can accompany defeat. The truth, however, remains: Our dreams mostly fail to see reality because we are content to allow them a resting place in our minds.

This world needs its dreamers. One of the race's chief failures is to dream listlessly and to follow the efforts of those who are satisfied to repeat the past. We need a better quality of dreamers, and we need more of them. Yet we need, even more desperately, those who are willing to work on, and for, their dreams. We need those who refuse to be content with the present and who willingly set their heads and hands to building the world their dreams demand.

These courageous souls will receive little praise, and too often they seem threatening. We, who claim to be realists, feel more comfortable with the glassy-eyed dreamer who does not expect much. The dreamers, however, who know that their dreams can find substance if they only labor, have a special claim upon the future.

An achievement is a dream realized. Twice blessed are those who dare to dream and dare to work.

❦   ❦   ❦

There is a "Very First Commandment." It is a prerequisite to all other commandments. It is: "Thou shalt believe in thyself." Without this, the others fall into disuse as empty cants.

It would seem a simple commandment, yet, because it is forgotten or ignored, there are those who find their days as well as their nights unending. Pressures everywhere attempt to strip us of confidence and leave us frightened and defenseless in a hostile environment.

Examples of such pressures are always near: Words which intimidate and shame, mischief which reduce others to commodities, lack of understanding between husband and wife, between parents and children, slurs, pitying glances, discriminating rules and laws, and on and on. Indeed, the list is almost endless.

There is, of course, no defense against these attacks — except the defense which can be built in the very core of our being. If, deep within our lives and minds, there is an uncompromising allegiance to the Very First Commandment—our confidence in ourselves—no remark, no action and no position can destroy us. We can be humbled, but not humiliated; beaten, but not defeated.

This is what the ancients taught when they told their startled listeners to love others..."as yourself." It's the "yourself" which was startling.

❦   ❦   ❦

Why are the busiest people able to accomplish so much while the others accomplish so little?

For the simple reason that the people with responsibilities are free. Those who have few responsibilities are not. Responsibilities demand a sense of order and discipline and create a sense of worth. Those "responsible" soon learn that they must organize their lives so that time is used efficiently. They understand that drifting time will only lead to the complaint: "What happened to the time?" Those with significant obligations create in themselves a sense of worth and a sense of freedom. They have done, and they can do.

Responsibility makes freedom viable. The important tasks, both in and out of the home, give a vitality to living which makes new options possible. We rarely know how much we can do—or how free we truly are—until the responsibilities accumulate. It would be well for those who claim they are "too busy" to examine and determine if their busy days are over-extended, or simply disorganized. Freedom comes not from the elimination of responsibilities, but from the elimination of jumbled procedures.

Sooner or later we all learn that clutter is not freedom, and laxity is not liberty.

The quest for freedom is a common search, and it will be found in the unexpected arenas of labor, service and thought. Freedom is not revealed in negligence. It hides in responsibility.

❦   ❦   ❦

He was a simple, direct, and hard working man. His talents were not outstanding. He was a craftsman, not an artist. The only defense of his labor and his only argument for being hired was: "I'll do the best job I can."

In an age of high pressure sales, of promises without results, of quick production and rapid turnover, these words ring like a clarion call. How very honest, how refreshing, and what a benevolent witness to the human enterprise!

That elementary phrase, words which do not require the usually obligatory "caveat emptor," says all that needs to be said about good salesmanship, or good human relations. Here, in the statement, "I'll do the best job I can," we have much of what we need to establish a better and happier world.

It is a great temptation to blame the problems of our time on the dehumanization of society, or the pressures of a fast-paced civilization, or the possibility of catastrophe. These are real problems. We, however, would be able to live far more easily with these difficulties if we could depend upon the fact that the mechanic, or teacher, or preacher, or politician would do the "best job he or she could." What kind of family, neighborhood, community or world might we have if all freely and eagerly subscribed to such a code?

"I'll do the best job I can," may not be one of the world's most elegant vows, but it's one of our finest.

There are few things as invigorating as impossible ideas. Take the most bland personality, add an impossible idea, and an amazing transformation will take place. The dull become exciting, the purposeless become directed, and the irrelevant become imbued with a sense of their own significance and possibilities.

Impossible ideas are everywhere, and they are free. Our friends have bountiful crops which they would love to share. Our enemies will be happy to contribute in the full belief that their impossible ideas will do us no good.

What wonderful things could happen if we would embrace that which "everyone knows" is impossible. Our difficulties could be turned upside down and backward. Our dull and routine tasks might undergo transformations if we thought "impossibly" about them. Artists, teachers, philosophers, and radicals of all kinds exist for the care and feeding of impossible ideas. They have always been around with impossibilities—and they changed the world.

The Queen of Hearts believed in "six impossible things before breakfast." Good for her! It might be a better world for all of us if we did the same.

CLOWN IN THE MIRROR

VI

*A more humorous attitude towards the
passing scene might make life more
bearable, and the ability to laugh at
oneself may be the final distinction
between the sane and the insane.*

There is a religious discipline which requires the practitioners to spend the first ten minutes of every day laughing. The purpose is to remind the faithful that much of life is laughable. We members of the "sit down, shut up and pay attention" generation could learn much from such an exercise.

One can't help wondering what would happen if we, as individuals and society, would look into the mirror some morning and burst out laughing. Instead of studying the serious countenance in the mirror, we might enjoy seeing a kind of clown staring back at us—and that might not be so bad.

We may find that life is much more rewarding when its not-so-serious side is recognized. After all, we are a pretty funny-looking species which spends much of its days in idiotic practices. This is not to say that our lives are wrong or unimportant to our fellow human beings, but rather to understand that our lives are not as serious as we have thought. A more humorous attitude towards the passing scene might make life more bearable, and the ability to laugh at oneself may be the final distinction between the sane and the insane.

We may not be able to laugh at the familiar clown in the mirror tomorrow morning, but we might begin with a quiet smile. What have we to lose?

❦ ❦ ❦

It is not difficult to bring fun into our lives, but it is a life-long task to find joy.

Fun can be bought. Games, thrills, and a variety of trinkets, from new cars to exotic toys, can be purchased. Our lives are constantly confronted with exciting displays which offer us chances to join other smiling people in fun. And we do buy and join! These quick breaks in the routine offer spice for otherwise dull days, and it would be cruel to deny our, or other's, needs.

But the cycle of fun is short. A quick moment of stimulation and then it is finished. We wear a forced smile when the roller coaster comes to a stop. There is a sadness in the air when the game is over, and our friends have gone home. It really doesn't take long for the new car to become "only transportation" or the clothes to become unfashionable. Fun arrives, contributes its brief sensation, and leaves.

Joy, however, is something else. More than a product of money, it is a product of effort, time and sacrifice. Paradoxically, it is both sought after and waited for. It is the goal of labor and stillness. It abides at birth and death. Joy is pried from the great stones of existence. It is the result of long hours, hours which included both frustration and despair. Joy often arrives at the end of a long, exhaustive effort, and occasionally it surprises us in the midst of effort.

Fun is escape which we all need; joy is fulfillment which we all seek. Fun is exciting, but joy is life. What a pity it would be if, in our quest for fun, we missed joy. What a shame it would be to have the good things, but miss the great things of life.

ᔆ   ᔆ   ᔆ

There needs to be time in each person's life for daydreaming: a few moments in each day when all the pressures and noises are put aside in order that we may simply drift. Every adult, like every child, needs the opportunity to do nothing and not feel guilty.

Daydreaming does not have status in our society. When caught in the act, we improvise some comment which will excuse the activity. We say, "I was making plans for tomorrow," or "I'm thinking about a particular problem." Rarely do we have the courage to say, "I wasn't thinking about anything—just daydreaming."

We live in a world of accomplishment. We are always expected to be doing something. There is a task to be done, dishes to be washed, letters to be written, chores to be finished, children to be cared for, and bosses to be pleased. There is seldom a time to watch a leaf flutter to the ground, gaze at drifting clouds, or just stare out the window. The demands of the clock and the weight of the burdens tolerate no alliance with daydreaming.

They should. Time and labor will drain us dry and leave us shriveled if we let them. It will take a daydream to refresh us. One of the ironies of life is that by doing nothing we equip ourselves to do something.

❦   ❦   ❦

Each of us has a story to tell. It may not be a new story, and some of the action may be as commonplace as the human experience itself. It is possible that our adventures may have been etched on ancient stones and many may testify that ours is "an old story." Yet we tell it because it is our story.

Those who keep their stories to themselves are few. We seem driven to approach our friends, and sometimes strangers, with our latest experiences. Something happened to us, and we want others to know.

This is the reason that "homecomings" and "reunions" remain popular. During the passing months or years we have garnered a new store of happenings and episodes which contribute to our tale. Accidents, incidents and milestones are added to the narratives of our lives until we are ripe for storytelling. Soon the words pour out of us, in a volume equal to the relationship, until the latest chapter of our continuing saga is complete.

The only thing we need at this point is someone who will listen to our story; someone whose interest and patience are significantly developed, and the only interruptions are leading questions. We need someone who will "hear us out," who will become neither drowsy nor testy, and who will be concerned with the outcome. In short, we need friends.

It is only when our story is finished that we learn the real price of friendship, for then we must listen to our companion's stories.

❦   ❦   ❦

The rainbow has long been used to illustrate the lessons and contracts of life, but the most significant lesson is its creation. The rainbow is born and exists on the battling edge of storm and sun. At the very point where rain and sunlight struggle for dominance, the rainbow appears. Rainbows do not exist in the midst of some violent downpour, nor do they fill the heavens on bright days. They are created at the meeting point of conflict.

The storms of life are crowded with fear, anguish and futility. It is sentimental in the extreme to suggest that we will someday look back on the tragic and sorrowful experiences and claim that they were beautiful. On the other hand, there are times when the joy of life is everywhere and all seems benevolent, but such is not the special environment of the rainbow. The rainbow is born in our lives when we've been through a storm and are emerging into sunlight.

A unique beauty is generated. Out of the struggle between dark and light, between the exhausting storm and exhilarating sunshine, a different kind of elegance and charm is created. The sorrow and pain are still present, but a new life is there also.

And if we haven't found a pot of gold, we simply have not looked in the right place.

❦   ❦   ❦

To agree to some burdensome or unattractive task is certain to gather praise from others and increase our sense of self-esteem. We are quick to praise those who respond to another's need. To do the unwanted and unappreciated is a sign of generosity and is deserving of accolades. Our individual lives are enhanced by such actions.

It, however, is not a betrayal of human decency or our sense of social obligation to say "No." We do a disservice to ourselves and others when we condemn such an honest and straightforward approach. There are times, and many of them, when our negative replies reflect self-awareness and maturity. It is important to understand that we do not betray our commitments when we say "No."

Nor is it essential to have a really good reason to renege. The fact that we don't want to do it, whatever "it" is, have better uses for our time and energy, or the simple recognition that it is not "our thing," are perfectly acceptable excuses.

Many of us are so accustomed to saying "Yes" to every request that the word "No" automatically triggers our sense of failure. On those rare occasions when we say "No" we immediately feel guilty. What a waste of guilt!

❧   ❧   ❧

"What do you do?" is one of the common questions. Even those who do not want to ask the question find that it is an obligatory topic at every social occasion. Postpone it as we might, it will surely find its moment.

If we have a desire to ask the question, it is equally sure that most of us want to answer it. During those rare conversations when the question is not posed, we wonder what the matter is. "Am I that uninteresting?" "Do they fear my answer?" "Does everyone already know?" We are eager to answer for the simple reason that by telling people what we do, we help them to understand just who we are.

Most of us are reasonably proud of what we do. When we tell one another what we do, we define ourselves. This definition establishes the context for further conversation, promotes the possibility of friendship, and articulates our own sense of worth.

This is why vacations are important. For a short period, we are not what we do. We simply are. In that moment when we are not what we do, we may come to understand who we are. Thus recognized, there are few situations as scary as vacations.

❧   ❧   ❧

Aesop taught us that familiarity breeds contempt. This, of course, is a partial truth because, while familiarity may breed contempt, the one thing it most certainly breeds is familiarity.

Our steady acquaintance with that which is near encourages us to notice warts and all. To complain about all those people and things which are part of our daily fare is our favorite sport. No house, no matter how beautiful, long escapes the probing eye of the inhabitant. No job, no matter how meaningful, maintains early enthusiasms. No avocation, no matter how initially entertaining, holds unwavering attention through decades. That which is familiar stands in immediate candidacy to become too familiar.

Nowhere is this more true than in families. The cute baby loses charm as diapers are changed again and again. The perfect student doesn't appear without flaws before parents. The famous and well-loved parent is inevitably a boor to offsprings. And, most noticeably, there has never been a spouse who could withstand the steady stare of the marriage partner. Even the strongest marriage betrays cracks upon close examination.

There is no answer to this dilemma. We will be familiar, and we will find fault. We cannot eliminate this reality, but we might reduce its intensity by occasionally moving far enough away to obtain a little perspective. At such a distance the children might appear more reasonable, the friends more attentive, the parents more worthy, and the spouse more attractive. We might learn what others see in them, and why distance makes the heart grow fonder.

❧   ❧   ❧

Shakespeare, as always, said it best: "All the world's a stage, And all the men and women merely players." True enough, but we are players who never got a chance to audition.

We, therefore, might be gentle with our fellow players.

We arrived on stage in the midst of an ongoing play, and so did they.

The curtain went up for all of us, and improvisation was the word of the day. This is a play where we make things up as we go along, and the performers and performances vary greatly. If we flub our lines and others interrupt, we should remember that a rehearsal would have helped and, besides, our fellow actors didn't ask for their parts either.

Each of us is truly unprepared. The casting director, working with a sparse budget and great time pressures, may not be terribly pleased with our performance, but what could be expected without an audition? Those judging our performance need to recognize that, given the lack of preparation and options, we are doing a pretty good job. We, itinerant actors performing in an improvisational play, are presenting no small amount of entertaining and cliff-hanging theater. We have a right to be proud of our performance.

And, let's face it, we may yet become stars.

❧   ❧   ❧

"How are you?" may be the most predictable greeting in our society. It springs from our lips without a thought, and we neither expect nor wait for an answer. Only extreme effort on our part allows the mind to recall those times when our question was answered with anything other than that most inoffensive of replies: "Fine." The greeting is seldom taken seriously.

Or is it? Perhaps the greeting isn't as trite and careless as cynics might have us believe. It is, after all, the basic concern of human society. The question does not seek to violate privacy or obtain information regarding some great and overwhelming subject, it simply establishes a note of interest and a realization that how we are is important to the community. As such, it is the proper question for a civilized and humane society.

"How are you?" is a question which is always more important than the answer. Our well-being will not be revised by our reply that "We are very tired," "We are aflame with new health," or "We are better since the operation." The greeting does not demand a reply other than the expected word, "Fine." It is the question, not the answer, which is vital.

"How are you?" is an expression seeking to establish a caring community. It deserves our participation; it is a mark of our humanity. The proper greeting for those who share this broken and frightened planet is the ever-popular "How are you?"

❦   ❦   ❦

Hypocrisy has justly received a bad name in the social circles of the concerned and honest. To name an act hypocritical or to call a person a hypocrite is to pronounce shame upon an event and warn others of a vile presence in our midst. To present ourselves as something we are not, to pretend to a belief which we do not hold, or to manifest a lie is to betray the confidence of society and twist the allegiances of our communities.

Yet hypocrisy may be turned in such a way as to create the beginnings of a new order. It is one thing to act falsely in an effort to court favors; it is quite another to behave differently from what we feel. It is one thing to act friendly when meeting face-to-face and then practice treachery at a distance. It is another thing to be pleasant even if we have no wish to encourage friendship. The first step in the reduction of animosity is an act of affability, even if we're not sure we mean it.

The most positive procedure for changing attitude is to change behavior. Our continuing failure, however, to recognize this simple fact causes untold heartache. In efforts to escape hypocrisy, we have blocked the most viable approach to understanding, that is, to change conscience by changing conduct. To act out what we do not feel and to say what we do not believe is never enough, but it could be a start.

We may not love one another, but would it be a terrible deed of hypocrisy to act as though we did?

❦   ❦   ❦

My good news is wonderful. Your good news is a bore.

That's a terrible thing to say, but isn't it true? We are thrilled when something good happens to us or our loved ones, and we are eager to tell others. But it is almost certain that their interest will be limited. A conversation about our good news will barely hold the attention of any but our closest friends, while a description of our bad news will capture the interest of strangers. Before we blame our friends and neighbors for thoughtlessness, we should remind ourselves how our mind wanders when we are regaled with the stories of a friend's good fortune or a grandchild's accomplishments.

The print and the electronic media are well aware that bad news sells while good news is left on the stands. We keep saying, "Why don't they tell the happy stories?" Would we buy them if they did?

Psychologists and philosophers will long argue as to why

we are attracted to bad news and spurn good news. It probably has something to do with our stage of evolution, or, at least, our emotional development.

We may have discovered a procedure for estimating our progress. When the time comes that others' good news is as interesting to us as our own, the human family will truly be advancing.

ꙮ   ꙮ   ꙮ

It was a retirement party, and the final speaker, the retiree himself, finished the evening by wishing that his friends, competitors, and successors might have fun.

It was an unexpected statement, but it expressed a vital element in all our lives. Why shouldn't we have fun? Why shouldn't that which occupies the work-a-day world encourage a good time? Where is it written that labor should be drudgery? Who profits by this unhappiness? It is time that we re-examine our various livelihoods and find ways in which they can be more enjoyable. We have nothing to lose but our melancholy.

Too often, we are so plagued by success, achievement or financial gain that we forget to have a good time. We are so busy trying to get to the place where we believe fun resides that we ignore the potential amusement in our lives. We labor so long and so unhappily to obtain happiness that we can't enjoy it once it is ours.

Life doesn't have to be that way. With a little insight and a goodly amount of courage, we can make changes. It all depends upon how we look at our labor, and how seriously we take it—and ourselves. After all, the rat race, the sweat shop, and the salt mine could be understood as:

competition, exertion and spice. Didn't those used to be the
ingredients for a good time?

❧   ❧   ❧

She was the most popular girl in the high school. When the
Homecoming Queen was elected, she was a shoo-in; when
the sophomores were chosen for the only sorority, it was
known that she would be selected; when classroom desks
were assigned, every boy prayed that his desk would be
near hers; when other girls had problems, they turned to
her for advice; and when the grades were printed in the local newspaper, her name led the list. So when he asked her
to the Senior Prom, and she accepted, he was scared
speechless. He had expected to be turned down, had made
proper plans to excuse his failure, and settle for a more
modest date. Now he was confronted with an achievement
beyond expectations, and fear was the natural product.
How does one handle the realization of fantasies, fame in
the midst of peers, and sudden awareness that you are out
of your league except with trembling hands and blurred vision?

How indeed? How do we in our adult world cope with
more-than-planned-for success? How but in fear do we
approach those great opportunities for which we had
longed and never expected? How do we behave when—
however it is presently understood—the prettiest girl or the
most handsome boy says, "Yes, I'd love to go to the prom
with you?"

There are times when fear is the natural and proper
emotion, and it comes not as a barrier but as a reminder
and stimulus. It reminds us that we are luckier than we

have a right to be, and that we can't stop now. It makes
life frightening—and wonderful.

There is no more futile statement than, "Don't worry
about it; there's nothing you can do." Such wisdom may
be well-intentioned, but it offers little relief. Of course,
we're going to worry over things about which we can do
nothing. That's why we worry! If we could do something
about the problem, we wouldn't be worrying. We worry
because there is nothing else to do.

Given, therefore, the inevitability of worry, we might try
to use it for some benefit. If we could understand worry to
be a careful consideration of a particular problem rather
than a prediction of the worst possibility, we might extract
some reward out of all this exhausting time. What is
needed is "directed worry."

If our worries could be transferred from fears to plans,
our time would be better spent. Rather than worrying
about our health, we might prepare our life so that it is
worthy regardless of our health. Rather than worrying
about our children, we could consider the options their actions make possible for us. Rather than worrying about an
arising difficulty, we might look at the problem "upside
down and backwards" and invent a solution.

Since we are going to worry, we might as well turn it to
our own advantage. It would be a shame to let all that
good energy go to waste.

The younger man asked his older companion, half in jest, "What is the secret for a long life?" The older man answered, and not so much in jest, "Luck."

It would be well for us not to dismiss the remark. Certainly some cynicism may have been present, and one should not discount the rules of safety and the guides to health. Yet luck does play a vital role. Who among us cannot count those whose lives were made substantial, or whose lives were cut short, by sheer chance alone.

As the whims of coincidence mar or make our lives, so they change our directions and our goals. When we enumerate those who assisted our achievements, we might be grateful and humble enough to list Lady Luck. She, also, made considerable contributions to our success.

The reality of chance should keep a rein on our conceit. Our desires and commitments may charm us into the belief that our labor will win the day, but it will also require luck. It therefore might be wise not to look too far ahead or to expect a guaranteed destination. Until chance has had its say, the future remains elusive and this should, at the very least, keep us humble.

❧   ❧   ❧

It is difficult to look at our world and laugh. Cry, yes; laugh, no. Problems ranging from fighting nations to fighting couples, from the battles between people of power regarding some imagined territory to the poorest of the poor who fight over empty bags, from businesses that participate in unfair practices to mail clerks who steal stamps, from teachers who challenge other teachers in order to ensure their place in line to children who cheat on unimportant tests, all go to portray a sad and unhappy world.

Given this state of sadness, we try to make our place by proving our importance. We tell ourselves that it is an unhappy world, but still, we are doing something important in it. We may be unhappy but we are unhappy for a good reason. This, we hope, will make the unhappiness tolerable.

We might profit from an entirely different approach. If we are aware that, in the long view, our obsession with importance will do little to reduce sadness, there might be hope. Surely we toil to lessen tragedies and struggle to diminish sufferings, but we know new tragedies will arise and suffering is immortal. Our earnestness needs tempering. For most of us, life is too serious to be taken seriously.

ꙮ   ꙮ   ꙮ

She was extraordinary. Here in a neighborhood grocery where others had gathered in various states of mess and haste, she was remarkable. Hair carefully combed, wearing coat, hat and gloves, she made a mockery of the far younger and naturally prettier women. She, alone among those in the store, was known by name, and this single acknowledgment seemed just.

Those who cared knew she lived around the corner in a dark, narrow apartment with a husband whose years had required more than their due. Decades must have passed since the last of the children left for brighter places. Now only the faded photographs and occasional letters served to unite the generations. The apartment with its lace curtains and worn chesterfield confessed an older and different, but not necessarily happier, time.

Here then, was a woman of years whose neighbors would have granted the relaxation of careless appearance.

She was no longer required to "make an impression" or "set an example." Those demands were long past.

But the inner drive was not stilled. The passage of time had left its mark of grace which would not be denied. She walked in quiet beauty and was a blessing to the day—a special blessing to the ragamuffins among us who wonder why an old woman would dress up "just to go to the grocery store."

❦   ❦   ❦

We have a right to be tired, but we rarely claim that right. We live in a society which is so obsessed with accomplishment, so mesmerized by the constant expenditure of energy, and so filled with admiration for those who labor far into the night, that we fail to recognize, or confess, exhaustion.

It is tempting to confuse fatigue with weakness. There is so much to be done, we are always in arrears with chores, and the world does await our saving efforts. We therefore refuse to admit the simple truth: I'm tired. Besides, there are those others who seem never to droop, and who reflect the Biblical injunction: "Run and not be weary...walk and not faint." Why can't we be like they are?

We simply don't realize that they also became exhausted. Supermen and superwomen are either characters in comic books or have learned to augment public alertness with surreptitious naps. Exhaustion may not be very attractive, but it is democratic.

Among the rights to be acknowledged, along with the noble declarations of religion, speech and assembly, let us affirm the right to be tired. And after we have acknowledged this right, let us have the humanity to reward it with the honor and rest it deserves.

🐦   🐦   🐦

The woman was young, probably in her mid-twenties, and there was little to draw attention to her. She would have been ignored had it not been for the way she crossed the street. She didn't walk, it was too fast for that, nor did she run as there was no obvious effort to gain time or exertion. She danced across the street.

This is not to say that the woman made some kind of exhibition of herself pirouetting across a thoroughfare. It wasn't a dance like one would see on a stage or share on some dance floor. This dance was simply a series of gentle leaps which gracefully moved the woman to music heard in her mind. It was entirely natural and must have been consistent with the young woman's approach to life and her own sense of style.

Most of us do not dance across the street and, given our talent and grace, this might be best. For us, crossing the street is simply a matter of need which is performed as effortlessly and as safely as possible. If we do not dance in such a situation no one would be either surprised or annoyed.

Yet there are others whose style, gifts and enthusiasm urge them to perform ordinary tasks in extraordinary ways. Rather than condemning them as "odd" or "show-offs," it might be good to simply rejoice in the differences. For some this may mean dancing across the street, for others it encourages different styles of clothing, for still others the differences are reflected in ideas, opinions or religions.

In every case the variety provides stimulation, reflection and, oftentimes, beauty.

We, of course don't dance across the street. It's not our style. But, then, what is our style?

❧ ❧ ❧

To exclaim, "I didn't know that," is to mark one of life's great moments. The very utterance is witness to the fact that something unknown is now known. Surely it is not too extravagant to claim that such an occasion is thrilling.

To learn: What a wondrous event that is! Somewhere back in the mists of time, one of our ancestors learned something. Who learned, or what was learned, is not ours to assess, but at that unrecorded moment human life assumed a new significance. It then required generations before our stumbling forebears realized that they had learned, and what a moment that must have been. When that ancient human being realized that he/she knew, the fabled gods must have stopped and gazed on such a marvel.

This, finally, is the great prize of our lives. Other gifts can be taken from us: our youth, our wealth, our profession, even our family and friends. Such losses will cause regrets, sadness, and abiding grief. But as long as we can learn, our days remain tolerable, even stimulating.

"I didn't know that," has never been judged as one of humankind's more noble utterances. It should be.

❧ ❧ ❧

Someone must have convinced magazine publishers that all people want to get rid of gray hair and wrinkles, for most of them carry articles and advertisements concerned with the obliteration of these evidences of life.

Why? Aren't those badges of living? Those hairs chronicle the days and events which have made our lives deep as well as long. The thrills of accomplishment, the sleepless nights, the nail-biting decisions, the pride of friend and family were part of the happenings which filled the days which, in turn, were accompanied by the steadily graying hair and extending wrinkles.

We realize that youth has its advantages—but not many. How sad it must be to always strive for the look of youth and long for those smooth-faced days, and not bask in the joy that comes from maturity and relish the fact that we continually live life. Eliminate those wrinkles. Why? They are ours; we have earned them.

We've labored hard for the years, the wrinkles, and the gray hair. Who are they who would deny us these honors of life? Would they have us pretend youth when age is that which is justly ours? If the lines in our faces note our follies there is no need for regret, they are part of us. If they illustrate our wisdom, we will take credit for that. We are no longer young, and that is not a crime. Nor is it a liability, unless we choose to make it so. The wrinkles, the gray hair, and the years are ours. We can be proud of them. Our age is our own.

SECRET TO SUCCESS

VII

Without plans and programs,
there is neither a sense
of direction nor an awareness
of progress.

What is success? For some, it is professional rank- ing, the automobile of one's dreams, or the vaca- tion of a lifetime. For others, it is riches, the won- derful house, or the achieving offspring. For a few, the quest for success is an excuse for rampant selfishness and irresponsibility.

But for others, and perhaps most, success is the wonder of living life in such a way that it is not necessary to walk on the face of a neighbor, or to share in the lies which pro- mote the accepted mythology. It is to be ourselves, not ob- sessed with impressing others, not to gloat over victory in some insignificant struggle. It is to find and follow the truth, and not to wonder how it will affect the anticipated promotion or the privilege gained by intrigue. It is to lay hold of time and arrange it according to the priorities which are cherished in private moments.

What is success? It is to be ourselves fully, openly, freely.

❦   ❦   ❦

How easy it is to hear. How difficult to listen. Sounds bounce against our ears all day: the noise of traffic, the clatter of machines, the steady steps on stair and sidewalk, the blare of radio and television, and the myriad voices.

Our loyal ears, in an attempt at self-defense, blot out these sounds lest our minds be driven into a pit of despair and anguish. We learn at an early age to hear but not lis- ten. It is a skill necessary for survival.

But there needs to be a time for listening and moments when we listen.

We know such moments when the artist fills our mind with music, and we become an open channel for beauty.

We know such moments when night gives way to dawn, and the first sounds of morning speak of new birth. We know such moments when the words "I love you" ring through the labyrinthine recesses of our being, reducing other sounds to silence. These, and many others, are our listening moments.

Listening demands much. The ears hear, but the whole being listens. Listening is not a simple mental exercise, it is a response. The listener feels the music, feels the sounds, and feels the words. To listen is not merely to pay attention, it is to have an experience.

In listening, we offer ourselves as receptive human beings to the art, concepts and yearning of others. Our artists, our companions and our children deserve nothing less.

❦   ❦   ❦

It is not simply doing a task which makes the effort worthwhile, it is doing the task well. Herein lies the secret of the fulfilled day and the procedure for self-esteem. Jobs are vital for a feeling of importance, but only those which are well-performed can provide a sense of worthiness.

Perhaps our society demands so many escapes and entertainments because we have lost the rewards which were the natural products of our labor and craft. To spend the day doing something only because "I'm paid to do it" or "Someone has to do it," and to labor without a sense of pride must be a good example of meaninglessness. The routine task done poorly, or with only an awareness of the passing hours, must be a fairly good working definition of hell. Surely this is an unhappy life.

The parent who tells the child, "Do whatever you wish, but do it well," is affirming far more than a reactionary demand or acting as the initial trainer for some later boss. The parent is conveying a vital truth: A duty or skill well performed is its own reward. The profits of industry and the price of production are far lesser values than the intrinsic reward which comes from an awareness that our efforts are shining extensions of ourselves.

There are those who claim that self-esteem is a prerequisite to achievement. This may be true, but equally true is the concept that achievement is a forerunner of self-esteem. In time we will learn that the well-performed task is a personal treasure and will remain so even when the consequence of our effort has turned to dust.

❦   ❦   ❦

History has rarely witnessed a member of the human race who didn't appreciate compliments. When we have labored diligently and used our talents well, words of praise are not only gratefully accepted, they are rightfully expected. We consider praise normal and proper.

What is less recognized, however, is the fact that we not only need praise, we need to praise. It is not enough for us to be the recipients of honor, we also need to be grantors of honor. To a great degree, our emotional health as a society and as individuals depends upon the existence of men and women worthy of praise and our willingness to praise them.

There is the desire in each of us to award those who have achieved. We need examples of excellence, we need assurances of quality, and we need acknowledgments of superior effort and enthusiastic dedication. There is a subtle, but vital, self-affirmation in the extension of praise.

Our lives would be dull and lonely if no one offered us praise. But life would be even more empty and futile if there were no one for us to praise. It is not enough to have the warmth of the sun. We also need the inspiration of the stars.

ಶ   ಶ   ಶ

Humility is a rare quality. We speak of it as a difficult virtue.

Humility should be a most common attribute for the simple reason that it is so natural. It requires no effort to be humble while, on the other hand, it requires an enormous expenditure of energy to be arrogant. Those who elect to exhibit arrogance have assumed the great burden of developing and defining little differences in life. Those who embrace arrogance must work many hours searching their talents and erecting their pedestals. Conceit, finally, is just plain hard work.

Humility, on the other hand, is convenient and uncomplicated. It is the affirmation that we share the vast majority of characteristics which mark members of our species. Only in minor ways are our fellow human beings physically or mentally our superiors or inferiors. While recognizing the unique qualities of each individual, the humble person knows that we share with the strongest and the weakest, with the wise and simple. This understanding makes humility not only possible, but is a natural posture for the human condition.

Arrogance is always an obsession with minutia. One who is arrogant must spend considerable energy drawing attention to some unimportant detail of his or her life, then employ additional energy to convince the impatient audience that the detail is crucial. What a waste!

How much more natural, and how much less painful it would be to affirm our vast communality. Humility would thus become a constant quality, and peace a possibility.

❧   ❧   ❧

Few among us can't recall times in our childhood when a comparison was used in the hope that it might reduce condemnation. It continues. Those are rare who do not seek the diminution of disapproval by comparing themselves with others. Students defend their grades, athletes defend their performances, artists defend their creations, parents defend their children, and merchants defend their practices by calling attention to their colleague's or competitor's greater weakness. "You think this is bad, you should see what Jimmy has done," is the common formula.

"Ethics by comparison" is an accepted practice, but hardly an honorable one. It proves nothing except the ability to evade, and that talent is in great supply.

It would be well for us to realize that such practices do nothing but reduce our sense of responsibility. As long as we believe that our actions are forgiven and our integrity left undamaged when defended with "ethics by comparison," we cheat ourselves. Such excuses only mean that we are not at the bottom...yet.

A vital, growing and defensible ethic demands not simply an acceptable performance but a challenging effort. Surely we want, and deserve, something better than simply getting by. The personal ethics of one's life shouldn't be a battered shoe which protects our foot from cuts and blisters, it should be a crown which we are trying to grow tall enough to wear.

❦   ❦   ❦

We smile when someone advises, "Plan your work and work your plan." It is such an old saw that it seems no more than a series of words which are hardly better than saying nothing at all.

Let us admit that it is an old saw, and let us go on to admit that it is a cliché and a platitude. Let us also admit that it is a practical note of advice which we fail to follow at our peril. Whatever this common bromide is, it is most certainly a realistic guide to human effectiveness. The sophisticated may smile at such a prosaic proverb, but those who seek efficiency will not ignore it.

Most of us have a problem with losing time. It's not that we waste time doing what society considers unproductive, it's not that we are self-indulgent and use the hours to pamper ourselves, it's that we suddenly find the time allotted us is gone and, for the life of us, we cannot account for it. Somehow we "lost" time. "Lost" time plagues us and renders our hopes and goals impossible. Without plans and programs, there is neither a sense of direction nor an awareness of progress.

The person who uses life well, who finds hours enough in every day, who accomplishes those things which others only dream of, and who discovers that the available energy is sufficient, is one who remembers and applies that ridiculous banality: "Plan your work and work your plan."

There is an ultimate gift. It can only be offered; it can never be requested. It is kindness.

We ask much. We can request mercy, generosity, graciousness, and understanding. We cannot appeal for kindness. We can demand honesty, fairness, and justice. There is no way for us to exact kindness. We can beg for assistance, plead for help, and even insist that we be recognized. No one can establish a claim for kindness, or even insist that it is due. Kindness is either extended or it is not.

When kindness is appropriate, the hesitancy is always there. It is noble to be driven by a sense of fair play. It is admirable to speak for the downtrodden and disinherited. It is essential that we extend the healing hand and the learned word. It is vital that we stand with and for justice. But the kind acts are neither so quickly embraced nor so publicly encouraged. Who will offer kindness?

This gift does not require that the donor be wealthy, educated or successful. What kindness does require, however, must be terrifying. How else can we account for its scarcity? Kindness should therefore be recognized as an act of courage, and the beneficiaries hardpressed to measure their gratitude.

❦   ❦   ❦

When we teach our children the art of giving, we also ought to teach them the art of receiving. Our embarrassments, apologies, and resentments which too often accompany the reception of gifts are just as ugly as selfishness, stinginess, and opportunism when it is our place to give. Denying another's gift is an expression of arrogance which says in bold terms, "I don't want you."

When a person receives, he or she establishes a bond

with the giver and, furthermore, the whole human race. To receive is to acknowledge that we do not live alone, we are not alone, we need each other, and we are dependent upon one another. Independence is a fine virtue, but interdependence is often a more realistic one. We depend upon one another and that mutual dependence is both affirmed and consecrated by the act of receiving.

The act of receiving is an act of graciousness, and a proclamation that we, too, are part of the human community. It is a willingness to understand that it is a blessing to serve and be served, an opportunity for others to repay long-standing kindnesses, and a notice that we care enough for others that we will allow them to come to our assistance. Receiving is a noble deed.

It is true that the ancient teaching affirms, "It is more blessed to give than to receive," but another lesson, equally old and honored, teaches, "Everyone that asketh receiveth." And receiveth graciously, we hope.

❧   ❧   ❧

Among the faults which are said to be especially noticeable in our present era—though it should be recognized that we have poor memories when we consider our faults—is the lack of punctuality. A persistent tardiness seems omnipresent. Only television shows, and airplanes for which we are late, appear to follow strict schedules. Even weddings, which once started on time as if the marriages depended upon it, now begin late.

For the most part this is not a major failure, and one could argue against being overly concerned with the dictates of clocks. Yet there are at least two failings which our tardiness reveals.

First, of course, we lack adequate organization. To be late betrays the fact that we are lax in our personal habits. Tardiness suggests that we are unable to rise with the alarm, that we dally over coffee, or simply refuse to abide by the order which, more than likely, we ourselves established. It may also convey the belief that we lack the fortitude to demand of others that they abide by our schedules in order that we might complete our tasks. As a result, a type of benign character flaw is exhibited.

Secondly, and more importantly, a lack of punctuality signifies that the one who waits is held in a secondary position. Whether designed or not, tardiness suggests that we keep someone waiting because someone else is more important. One who is regularly tardy should remember the old French proverb: "Men count up the faults of those who keep them waiting."

❦   ❦   ❦

Although dictatorships are universally denounced as a proper form of government, there is a dictatorship of the self which is absolutely essential. Without this type of inward despotism, we are unfocused and stumble our way through life. There can be no success, regardless of how that word is interpreted, because there is no consistency by which one can gauge achievement. There is no responsibility because the actions do not follow a predictable, not to mention heedful, pattern. There is no love because the unwavering concern for another is absent. In short, when one assumes and exhibits a freedom from the inner directions of conscience and commitment, the person is not only irresponsible, he or she is also deranged.

Commitment is an unappreciated word in our society.

We would much rather talk about freedom. Freedom, however, comes from the environment, whereas commitment demands action. We are free to choose our commitment, but in that commitment we elect both to use and to limit freedom. The self-imposed dictatorship of the soul may seem frightening, but it is the chief defender of justice, the creator of beauty, and an essential ingredient in love.

Ages ago an itinerant teacher told his followers that they were free to choose a master. They couldn't choose two or three, they had to choose one, and that one they would serve. This is still true.

❦   ❦   ❦

There had been a long discussion of ethics, with serious thought given to the extent of participation in what could have been a dangerous situation. The questions were vital and each person was weighing obligations, expectations and fears, when one man, perhaps more gifted than the others, said, "The worst a person can do is to kill me, and I'm not afraid to die."

Here was one who cut through to the nub of the issue, understood that fear of death was the debilitating factor, and decided that he was not afraid to die. Once this concept was articulated, other decisions fell into their natural place.

Until the fear of death is raised to the level of consciousness, it lives in the shadows and can be mistaken for a greater villain than it is. When each of us becomes acquainted with our own fear of death, we bring it into the open air of our lives. If we fail to confront our fear, it becomes a lurking phantom.

Such a suppression can be destructive, but worse is the result which can be delivered because others use our fear. If we believe that our individual death is the ultimate tragedy, then we become the potential victims of any demagogue or mob. Our fear of death, or the lack of it, will do much to determine the shape and strength of our character.

An act of courage is not so much the result of outward strength as it is a product of inward resolution.

❦   ❦   ❦

"When you find anything monotonous," the old priest said, "keep at it five or ten minutes longer."

Such advice is almost sure to be ignored. If there is one consistent factor in our society, it is the pledge that life should not be boring. We surround ourselves with stimuli guaranteeing that, if any monotony threatens, we will move to another entertainment immediately. Heaven save those people who, either because of birth or style, prove uninteresting, for they shall be ignored. Our entertainment-seeking culture will not tolerate the tedious.

Therein lies a loss. The great virtues of life—love, tolerance, patience, understanding—are rarely the products of instantaneous revelation. They become ours only after we have travelled to the far side of boredom. The poem emerges slowly out of the mounds of wasted paper, the experiment releases its truth only after the failures have become legion, the decision is secured more often during the fortieth conversation than the first, and wisdom shares its beauty only with those who have learned to appreciate grey prose.

We are often told that such and such a task is a bore. If

that is so, we may have received notice of its importance. Staying with it five or ten minutes longer, we may learn a great truth, or at the least, a great discipline—which is almost as good.

❧   ❧   ❧

The evening's lecturer was a highly respected religious leader who was noted for having established successful religious communities which promoted the enlightened development of both individuals and societies. While he was not a member of the more popular religious cultures, his opinions were listened to carefully, especially by the younger members of his audience. A sense of shock, therefore, went through the audience when he told a questioner that one of the chief contributions and marks of a truly religious person was...neatness!

In an age in which a kind of slovenliness had become vogue and careful attention to one's attire and living habits was believed to be hopelessly materialistic, it was stunning to hear this spokesman for an "alternative life style" promote neatness as a quality greatly to be desired.

There should have been no surprise. The orderliness of one's exterior life is a good sign of the orderliness of one's interior life. How we maintain our person is an adequate revelation of what we believe about ourselves. The efficiency with which we handle our chores and arrange our desks is an indication of the importance we place on our jobs and fellow human beings.

Neatness is not one of the traditional commandments, but it is a statement about ourselves, and what we say about ourselves always precedes what we say about our faith. No wonder the religious leader called for neatness. So might we all.

From time to time it is good to resurrect a word which is thought to have been outgrown. In recent years the word "play" is used as often by theologians as by children. "Games" has proved to be a word as common among psychiatrists as among neighborhood boys. We, undoubtedly, could add others and included in those we may find that old standby: "Discipline."

When we were growing up, "discipline" was what parents did to keep us well-behaved, or was a synonym for work and study. Many of us hoped that "discipline" would be among the "childish things" we could put away when we became men and women. Yet our lives prove that we didn't outgrow the word and now, long after the threat of "discipline" has disappeared, the concept has become more relevant than ever.

While it continues to be true that we resent the "discipline" forced upon us by others, a "self-discipline" is vital for the creative evolution of our lives. If we wish to open doors and expand horizons, there is no substitute for discipline.

The word "discipline" wasn't one of our favorite words when we were children and may not be one of our delights today, but ironically, and belatedly, we may find it as a guide and path to joy.

There is no tempter more ruinous than procrastination. To succumb to this temptation is not only to be led astray, but to do so without even the thrill of having performed some foolhardy or immoral act. Procrastination fails to grant so much as a shameful memory. We are fortunate if the task which we had put aside did not become more burdensome in the meantime. Unlike more attractive tempters, procrastination has no redeeming qualities.

We have known the liabilities of "putting things off" since we were children. Few of us do not retain childhood memories of the wasted time, the whining, the dawdling, and the outright lies which were part of our early years. As we grew older and more sophisticated, we employed more complicated approaches to our maturing procrastination. We learned to feign illness, ignore, and, most importantly of all, argue. Rare are those men and women who do not remember that ringing parental admonition: "Stop arguing and just do it!"

As it has turned out, that was a wise command. It was too bad we didn't embrace it; it is too bad that we don't embrace it.

❦　❦　❦

The two friends had not seen each other for several years and following the usual comments about health, the state of the world and concern about one another's family, the common question was asked: "What are you doing these days?" The answer was quick in coming: "Trying to learn one more new thing; in fact, to learn something new each day is about all I try to do at my age."

For any age, that is a good answer. To learn one new thing each day is challenge enough for any stage of life, any degree of status, any real or imagined position among one's peers. Before we are strong enough to labor, or when we are no longer strong enough to labor; before our fingers are trained to manipulate pen on paper, or after our eyes are too weak to read what other pens have written; in days when we were not skilled enough to walk, or in years when such skill demands more than its due; there is time to learn something new each day. Life requires much, and it gives much. From the beginning, there are new things to see, new sounds to hear, new foods to taste.

Whatever may be denied, there is always something to be learned. No loss is so great, no view so limited, no darkness so deep, that a quiet voice within does not say: "Learn! Learn!"

One of the great joys of human existence is to lay one's head back on the pillow at the end of a long day and pass into sleep while recounting what has been learned since awakening.

YOU MAY BE RIGHT

VIII

It takes a great deal of personal security

to allow an adversary.

The letter was complete with wise comments regarding the human situation, but it also contained a remarkably practical quotation: "If you have two cups and two plates, you need never be lonely."

One may choose to be alone, and there are times when the solitary venture is necessary. But there are other times when we find ourselves alone and lonely, and these are the situations we elect to avoid. Fortunately, the vast majority of us do not need to be lonely, and company is as close as the cordially offered invitation.

We, of course, may choose not to offer the invitation. Excuses are ever at hand: The house is not neat, there hasn't been time to bake, illness has just left or is threatening, and there is always the weather. When this is the case, however, we should be honest with others and ourselves and either admit that we enjoy being alone or prefer to obtain attention by complaining. In our straightforward moments we know full well that there is no reason for our loneliness, but once we slide into the quicksand of self-pity it's tempting to stay there.

The statement, "If you have two cups and two plates, you need never be lonely," is a bare truth which many of us will find difficult to accept, but it is the answer to loneliness. It would be wise for most of us, during those days when the loneliness seems especially severe, to take an inventory of our cups and plates and see if we can't find an answer to our problem.

❦　❦　❦

"Gentlemen," the wise professor said to his eager class, "if you can't see the bottom of the stream it may be that the stream isn't so very deep, it's so very muddy."

This perceptive remark should hold a prominent place in our minds because most of us are too quick in confusing befuddlement with wisdom. We often mistake another's muddled thinking for our own lack of ability. More than once we have berated ourselves for a failure of intellect when, in fact, the failure belonged to the one whose lack of preparation befogged the situation.

Some subjects and systems are best communicated to a select group. But these are isolated and protected involvements. Problems and possibilities which are the proper concerns of the masses should be readily grasped. To claim that a development is too complicated for general appreciation, especially when it affects the lives of that same general public, is to project an arrogance which should give rise to various fears.

Our confession that we do not understand is not a revelation of stupidity, it announces that the effort to communicate failed. The person attempting to explain has a responsibility to communicate, just as the listener has a responsibility to concentrate. If we do our part and still do not understand, it might be well for the teacher to return only when he or she is more adequately prepared.

Understanding is a two way process, and requires both a student who makes an effort and an instructor who makes the effort worthwhile.

❦   ❦   ❦

When H.L. Mencken would receive an especially hysterical letter denouncing one of his opinions, he would occasionally reply with the simple one line statement: "You may be right." Not only was this an immensely logical retort, not only did it meet the Biblical counsel, "a soft answer turneth away wrath," but it affirmed Mencken's belief in himself and his position.

It takes a great deal of personal security to allow an adversary. Most of us are so insecure that we must convert the world to our belief. The existence of a single non-convert seems a threat. The managements of some large business corporations consider the rejection of one resolution in a list of twelve or fifteen resolutions to be a vote of "no confidence."

Would that more had the confidence to say, "You may be right." Such a statement contains no denial of our commitment, nor is it a rejection of our resolve; it is a thoroughgoing affirmation of another opinion and a declaration that our position is not shaken by another's right to disagree.

How many useless arguments we would save and how many hours of anguish and doubt we would escape if, by the witness of our assurance, we could look into the eyes of our detractors and say, "You may be right." And, as an unintentional by-product, we might open a few closed minds.

❦ ❦ ❦

He hung up the phone with a sigh. It was a sigh which had passed his lips many times. A trip to the files, a quick search for the right folder, and then to empty it in the wastebasket: the final act. Months of concern were over, there was nothing left to do, he must now forget and be about his business.

Yet these acts seemed so harsh, so unfeeling. The correct words had been uttered, the letters written, and there was nothing more to do. The empty file folder was an adequate symbol that the case was closed and the process of forgetting was in gear. He knew that these procedures are efficient and in a few months, or a couple of years at most, the events and names would be erased from memory.

There is bitterness in knowing that there are times when the chief healing force in life is not memory, but forgetting. There are limits to our talents and the weights we can bear, and the act of forgetting is the natural process which saves us from being exhausted or breaking under the strain.

Certainly, we feel guilty when well-known signs tell us that a tragedy is about to be forgotten or another's problem is to be buried in oblivion, but failure to do so would soon sacrifice us on an altar of sorrow. And not to forget, not to go about our new business, would imprison us in the griefs of the past and render us useless as we seek answers to the present and its fresher heartbreaks. There are times when we serve best by forgetting, and occasions when the words, "I have forgotten," are a confession of our continuing sanity.

❦   ❦   ❦

Tradition—a tradition supported by much scholarship—holds that the Buddha's final words to his disciples were: "Work out your salvation with diligence." Or, as it is often poetically stated, "Be ye lamps unto yourselves, be your own confidence."

The ancient voice from the East speaks ably to the West. It makes little difference whether we are Asian or European, rich or poor, intellectual or illiterate; the temptation for all is to seek another who will guide us, another who will be our "lamp."

There is ample reason for this. Few could live many years without being battered by existence. When problems seem to dash our most cherished hopes, it is natural that we seek someone or something who will do for us what we either cannot or will not do for ourselves.

But the words of the Buddha ring down through the centuries. They do not claim that life is easy or that our difficulties are imaginary. The ancient wisdom teaches that no one can solve our problems or relieve our pain but ourselves.

❦   ❦   ❦

Each generation, including our own, is tempted to believe that its own era is unique. Assuming that no one has thought, believed or feared as we, we build a new altar for the worship of the contemporary. But is our uniqueness fact? Have we moral insight superior to earlier generations? Are today's critics more essential or forlorn than those of an earlier century? Like the teenager who cannot believe that his mother or father ever knew a love as all-consuming as his, we assume that we are unprecedented.

When we subscribe to the arrogance of the contemporary, we isolate ourselves from the sweep of history and its lessons. We assume the mantle of rampant self-importance and affect a conceit which is both a private nuisance and a public liability.

Surely there are problems unique to our age, and there are achievements which are wonders, but the earlier eras were not vacant, and their wisdom shines afresh. Those who would speak vitally to the present time would do well to study other times. Here, too, the race suffered, hoped, struggled and survived. Our problems bear our names, but they are not new; our solutions carry our reflections, but they also bear the mark of the past. The arrogance of the contemporary is tempting, and like other tempters, it plays the victim for a fool.

🐛 🐛 🐛

It was a plain and earnest request: "Please remember me in your prayers." And we answered, "Of course." But what does this mean? Her need was clear, and her adversary deadly. The march of natural process was inevitable.

We children of such a scientific and sophisticated age can hardly believe that prayer is a device which will cause the forces of nature to reverse themselves. Could we argue with the Almighty or lay claim to some unique persuasion? Of course not.

Prayer is neither superstition nor magic. It is an act by which we place another's burden in the center of our consciousness. Prayer, in whatever context, is always a deliberate function of personal involvement. It is to gather the myriad needs and fears of another into our active reflection, and in some quiet space consider and respond. It may be that to pray for another reflects the religious tradition of the one who prays, but even those who claim no tradition, by accepting the request to pray, convey a feeling of love and respect which cannot be denied.

To say to one in great need, "I will remember you in my prayers," is to convey notice that their difficulty will be our constant concern, and we will remember them until resolution and peace finally arrive. It remains true, even in our age, that to be remembered in prayer is a precious gift.

It is a temptation for us to read into another's suffering or sorrowing our own feelings. When we are confronted by the person in pain or sorrow, we assume that he or she feels as we would feel.

How many times we have visited the bedside of the ill and, without consciously doing so, supposed that we knew how much the afflicted was suffering. And how many times we have been wrong!

The mistake was born of the fact that we are observers and not participants. There is an emotional and intellectual barrier between us: the experience of the observer and that of the sufferer. We do not know what subtle and vital changes are being experienced in the inner recesses of the mind.

We need to be cautious when evaluating another's condition. Much harm may be caused by our assumptions. It is possible to make our own lives a living hell by assuming feelings which do not exist or by speculating upon fears which are ours and ours alone. Even here the ancient words ring true: "Judge not."

❧   ❧   ❧

Our dictionary informs us that a cliché is a "trite phrase; a hackneyed expression." It is; but before we allow criticism full rein, we should remember that a cliché is also a truth. No doubt it is a truth which has become so familiar as to be invisible and unheard, and its edges are worn smooth by years of handling, yet its truth cannot be denied.

Can we remember the first time we heard what we now know as a cliché? The insight and clarity gave us pause. Our thoughts rode on the back of a revelation. The first words that entered our consciousness were, "Of course," and "How right." In that initial encounter, we found inspiration and beauty. Such wisdom had earned the right to be a cliché, for it was, and is, a significant and old truth.

Perhaps we need to recycle clichés. The years have made us sophisticated, and we turn and snicker when someone utters one of these "trite and hackneyed expressions." We are above all that now. Or are we? It may be that those worn words and tired phrases still have a mite of encouragement for us—especially those of us who are so sure that we outgrew such things years ago.

We might try, for starters, recycling that old cliché: "Every cloud has a silver lining." It's threadbare, dog-eared and badly scuffed from years of overuse. It's almost worn-out, but one fact remains: It happens to be true.

❦   ❦   ❦

Many people were greeting the young man following his dramatic presentation. Among the early well-wishers was a former professor who, though noted for his abrupt manner, was generous with his praise. The young man, obviously impressed by his mentor's compliments, stammered, "Well, sir, I don't know how to respond." The professor answered sharply, "You say, 'Thank you!' That's all you need to say."

"Thank you" is often all we need to say. These two words carry a remarkable message, and familiarity does not diminish their importance. In our efforts to be gracious and appreciative, we devise an array of responses which we hope will convey the totality of our gratitude. It is rare, however, for such complicated ceremonies to profess as much gratefulness as those two simple words: "Thank you."

Parents who taught their children to say, "Thank you,"
may have been old fashioned, but they were not thoughtless. "Thank you" remains a mark of graciousness and
civilization. It provides us with a point of common humanity, and confesses our need and respect for one another.

After we have sung our finest song, painted our most
beautiful picture, and whispered our most tender words,
the phrase, "Thank you," will be heard. It will be enough.

❦   ❦   ❦

It began a long time ago when we were given a slice of
cake and wanted it all, or when we had to share a toy and
the cooperative venture was not what we had in mind, or
when a parent went away and we wanted that parent with
us. Always it seemed that there was someone nearby, and
someone supposedly smarter than we, who told us that we
couldn't have it all. The years rolled by and we grew big-
ger and older, but there continues to be some recognizable
authority telling us: "You can't have it all."

We've learned to live with this truth. Not graciously perhaps, but tolerably. We still want it all, and always someone—though now it is more often something—informs us,
"You can't have it all."

What are we to do? We could, as we once did, cry,
shout, and throw a tantrum. But few will be impressed. Or
we might, as we have done on occasion, pout and say, "I
don't want any of it if I can't have it all." Unfortunately,
such an attitude is certain to leave us empty-handed. If we
want it all, we are in trouble.

So we wisely compromise. If we can't have it all, we can
learn to settle for, and be satisfied with, what we can have.
The earth, the opportunities, the benefits, and love are all

in short supply. We can't have it all, but we can have part of it, and we learn that a part is enough.

One of the beneficial aspects of maturity is an awareness that we neither want nor need "it all." That gives a vital new meaning to the old expression, "Enough is enough."

❦   ❦   ❦

Of all the arts available to humans, words may be the most significant. They can be used to enlighten or confuse, to charm or accuse, to reveal or conceal. They have ignited wars and promised peace.

In the mouths of the plain-spoken they can be a confession of honesty. Clear words in crisp phrases can eliminate doubts and lay bare the deeper feelings and thoughts.

Among the more conniving, however, words can be shaped and twisted so that they reveal nothing at all. Anticipating the desires of the hearer, the word-artist can produce a line of syllables to flatter and obscure. With careful attention to lexicon, the enemy can be camouflaged to resemble a friend.

Those who seek allies in their search for the fuller life must not confuse the word with the deed. The word-artist can affect a new vocabulary and, like a gifted chameleon, change color without changing place. To seek assistance, support or understanding on the basis of words used or unused, is to court disappointment and tempt disaster.

It continues to be true: Every tree is known by its own fruit—not by the way wind rattles through its leaves.

"I'm sorry," is the first step in both reconciliation and growth. To say, "I'm sorry," is to recognize that an act has been performed which has hurt another and affirms that an effort is being made to rectify the situation. The phrase also announces that another human being stands ready to provide assistance for the next act in life's drama.

It may be that "I'm sorry" is a confession of guilt and synonymous with an apology, but such is not always true. There are events in our routine lives in which pain is inflicted without any intention of harm. Still the pain is there, and our words can be an attempt which marks the possibility of a new beginning. To say, "I'm sorry," when meeting a friend who has just suffered a loss is more than a sympathetic greeting, it is notice that we stand ready to do all within our power to help and encourage.

"I'm sorry" may sound weak and uninspired when it leaves our lips during times of pain and sorrow, but such is a beginning. There will be a time when a quiet peace will mend the torn spots and repair the ragged edges, or there will come a new dawn which overtakes the night. But, first, "I'm sorry."

❦ ❦ ❦

There are occasions when it is invigorating to "fight a battle." Situations do arise when a wrong needs to be righted or a procedure needs sustaining. Whether one wins or loses, there is a certain feeling of accomplishment in the struggle.

There are other times when the rewards, even in victory, are for naught. We all have experienced those episodes in which we have done our best, lost, and been depressed.

Still more depressing, however, are those battles which we may have lost, or even won, and have come away with the full knowledge that the effort wasn't worth it. The whole thing was a waste of time.

Knowledge of when to do battle may be one of wisdom's chief marks. An awareness of when to fight and when to forget it is an essential ingredient in living an accomplished and self-accepting life. There are times when it is necessary to fight the good fight, and there are times when it is vital that we ignore the foolish fight. Fools never learn the difference, but those who know which is which are victors even before the battles begin.

❧   ❧   ❧

In the Qur'an, the holy book of Islam, we read, (and it is repeated in several passages) "We will not task the soul beyond its ability." While recognizing the position of the soul in Islamic theology and the dynamic relationship between the soul and its Creator, this ancient message still encourages secular considerations.

It is a rare person who does not "push too hard." We do not simply task ourselves too severely, we feel guilty because we cannot accomplish the impossible. It may be that such an attitude was developed in response to goading, if well-intentioned, parents. It may be that when we were children we felt ashamed because we could not do the things which we simply could not do, and as adults we are remorseful because we cannot accomplish the inconceivable.

Society suffers from a plethora of those who feel guilty because they cannot perform miracles. Enough! We need

no more of them. What we need is what we've always
needed: Men and women, boys and girls, who will perform
those tough and thorny tasks which reside in the realm of
the possible.

The Qur'an teaches: "We will not task the soul beyond
its ability." Secular civilization might reflect on such wisdom and decide: "We will not task ourselves, our neighbors, or our children beyond their abilities."

❦   ❦   ❦

"Say the magic word." Who among us can't remember
that command? We heard it as children; we repeat it as
adults. The word "Please," is, in truth, a magic word.

It was magic to us as children because it transformed in-
action into action. Our request was issued, and nothing
happened. Then, either through demand or memory, we
said the magic word and the arrested world came alive. As
adults we hear the appeals of youngsters, and we reply,
"Say the magic word." We sometimes surprise ourselves
with the strength of our position and fully realize that we
are quite prepared to deny the request if it is not accompanied by, "Please."

In truth, civilization will not fall, nor will a child's true
needs be denied, if the magic word is not uttered. This is
not a matter of world-shaking or life-threatening consequence, but it is not a matter to be slighted either. "Please"
is one of those words which assists in the establishment of
civility. It's not necessary for survival, but it may be necessary for making survival comfortable.

"Please" enables the human community to be more considerate, more gentle, and more humane. When you come

to think about it, and how easy it is to be thoughtless in our world, maybe "Please" is a magic word. In fact, it may be more than magic, it may be miraculous.

❦   ❦   ❦

Human beings have remarkable recuperative powers. Confronted with stunning failures, disappointed, and afflicted by devastating tragedies, we still recover—often with a new understanding of ourselves and our neighbors. The student of human nature soon learns that men and women are not readily crushed by misfortune.

What does take a toll, however, is the "everydayness" of life. The routine, habits, and boredom of day in, day out existence wear away human consciousness and induce pain where tragedy cannot touch. Those who have withstood the worst that a malignant evil had to offer are sometimes destroyed by the benign efforts of daily monotony. That which was heroic in the face of disaster can be destroyed by tedium.

We take pride in overcoming the evils which marred the lives of our forebears, and we have a right to that pride. None should doubt that ours is a safer world. But even with the great evils to battle which are still before us, and a conviction that we will ultimately triumph, the task of making the daily grind meaningful is our immediate struggle. To conquer boredom, transform monotony, and breathe new life into the world-weary still awaits.

The struggle against "everydayness" is monumental because of its constancy and, when destroyed, its tendency towards resurrection. To continue the ongoing fray and maintain our commitment to self-preservation, even as we

aid those who have been wounded in the same struggle, is
to be an everyday hero. And that's the best kind.

❦   ❦   ❦

It is hard to listen to both sides of an argument. There is
something very untidy about the process, and we are always left with much personal work. It is so much easier to
get on a bandwagon and assume that we are right.

But there is no substitute for this hard work. The old
saw "There are two sides to every issue," is one of the
more unpopular clichés, but it is true nevertheless. To hear
that other side, just when we thought we had all the information and our minds were settled, is a weighty task. How
much more simple life, especially our lives, would be if the
"other side" would do us a favor and go away.

Of course, it won't go away, and it must not. To listen to
that other side is the basic ingredient of that ancient and
essential value: Justice. If we refuse to listen to both sides,
if we are sure that we know the truth and "we don't need
to hear any more," then Justice is sacrificed and our lives
are the less for it.

Confidence is an attitude which is much respected in our
culture, and for good reason. But if Justice lives, the opinions which we have not considered must be heard. And
more personally, each of us needs the confidence to tell
ourself : "I could be wrong."

❦   ❦   ❦

From time to time, each of us meets a person who is so
physically attractive we have a difficult time concentrating
on the topic of our conversation or paying attention to the

subject that was expected to be our primary interest. We are tongue-tied and often see ourselves as clumsy and foolish. Handsomeness has a way of inflicting powerlessness.

Days later we still find ourselves reflecting upon these encounters and chastising ourselves for not saying something bright which might have redeemed us. In these later times we inevitably think of some witty or wise comment which would have reduced our discomfort.

It is true that authentically beautiful people make us uncomfortable. This may be the primary reason we, in spite of our better natures, are quietly pleased when those people have public problems or their beauty fades. Good looks may be an asset, but it is also a burden.

Better than beauty is charm, which may or may not accompany handsomeness. Beauty is a gift which could become a handicap, but charm is an achievement which promotes benefits. Beauty encourages compliments; charm encourages companionship. As Adlai Stevenson once said, "A beauty is one you notice; a charmer is one who notices you."

Beauty and charm are locked in an eternal battle. Beauty will win the eyes, but charm will win the mind. Beauty will look great tonight, but charm will be wonderful in the morning.

AWARE OF THE MOMENT

IX

For everything, and everyone,

there is a season.

It's September and the mind wanders back in time. No matter how hard we try to ignore them, memories crowd our minds: Wide-ruled tablets, freshly sharpened pencils, the smell of newly oiled floors or newly painted classrooms, and the feel of something new, books, ribbons, dresses, and shoes. The thrill of something new to learn, the wonder about the new teacher, the tingle that recalls the schoolyard infatuation, the fear of playground battles, and the excitement that is the new school year, all are present.

How many years has it been? Who knows? Who cares? It is September and our world is awash with possibilities. It is autumn, perhaps the autumn of our days, but still the springtime of childhood and youth have grasped our minds and refuse to be denied. Attempts to affirm our mature days, efforts to prove that we are no longer attracted by ancient Septembers, labors designed to concentrate attention on the present, all prove futile. Will we ever grow up? Probably not. There is something within us that wants the new book, the new class, the new idea, the new chance. We may find solace, comfort and stability in the past, but we are not satisfied to settle there. Something inside us seeks opportunities. We want to try something. We want to be something new.

We remember September, and memories stir. It is an old schoolyard feeling, but will we deny it? Never. Not even for all the peanut butter sandwiches and chocolate chip cookies in your lunch box!

❧   ❧   ❧

For most of us, New Year is a time of rejoicing. The Jewish New Year, however, is not necessarily a festive time. While

165

recognizing that there are festive occasions within the context of the High Holy Days, this day is essentially for reflection, confession and penitence.

Within Judaism there is a lovely metaphor regarding the Book of Life, and these Holy Days provide the Jew with an opportunity to examine that book. Each person, in reality, is the author of his or her own life, and needs to consider what should be kept, and what should be thrown away. This New Year says, "Look at the Book of Life, your Book of your Life, and see what mars its pages, what defiles its beauty, what corrupts its potential; then clean that page, erase that trespass, start afresh."

All of us, Jew and Gentile, write in our Book of Life. In it the debits and credits are kept more accurately than those maintained by any biographer, any accountant, or any tax agent. We know when we have performed deeds of meanness and spoken words of hate. There needs to be a time to reflect on these things, to seek forgiveness, and to cast out.

Before the book closes, there are things to be done; things to be said. Then, like one who has read words of great wisdom, and been revealed in a poet's metaphors, we may rise to go about our days afresh. These are the days of our own new year.

❦   ❦   ❦

Yom Kippur is an opportunity for every Jew to focus attention upon her or his own life. It is a time of such importance that not even food should interfere.

The universal lesson in this holy day is to understand that the focal point is not some historical issue or some planetary problem, but the life of which the individual is the center. The person sitting in synagogue or home has only one issue to consider: her or his life. Tradition and Law are clear for the Jew on this day. You are the topic, and you have control over your life. No one knows what you know, has been where you have been, or has done what you have done. No one can do for you what you must now do for yourself.

On this holy day there should be no interruption in order that the solitary man or woman might do what he or she alone can do. The international events, the struggle for justice, the neighborhood improvement, and even the preservation of the synagogue or Judaism itself are unworthy temptations. This is the holy time for the individual to face the reality which is finally hers or his. There is no more holy labor.

To see ourselves as others see us is a curious wish. To see ourselves as only we can see ourselves is an incredible and sacred concept. No wonder Yom Kippur is called a Day of Awe.

❦   ❦   ❦

It is necessary to be careful lest we turn autumn into a season of runaway sentimentality. All admit that there is a startling beauty to these weeks with the exciting color of the leaves. This pageant includes the very last tree, so reluctant to lose its sere foliage. Lyricists seem especially fond of the season, and they never tire of extolling this wonderful time. Even leaf raking—perhaps the most futile of all yard chores—gains its share of nostalgia-based compliments.

What is autumn, really? It is the end of growth, the retreat against the oncoming winter, the withdrawal of life support systems which in earlier times provided birth, growth and maturity. Autumn is nature's exiting season.

But it does go out in style! Instead of a sudden loss of life with appropriate colors of brown and gray, we are treated to yellow, red and orange—as if the meadow's spring flowers had been reincarnated on the trees' branches and the hillsides. Unwilling to accept the inescapable fate with melancholy, the green of summer becomes the colorful autumn, and the dying is transformed into a recollection of spring's beauty and a promise of what lies beyond the winter snows.

Here, in the midst of death, is a lesson on how to die. It is a lesson for all.

❦   ❦   ❦

There are at least three Halloweens: The one which is concerned with the religious aspects of All Hallows Eve and Day, the one which fascinates children and tempts teenagers, and the one which stimulates the imaginations of all ages. It is this latter concept which is inescapable.

Imagination fills the gaps left by the ordinary. Life, finally, may not be as mysterious or as colorful as we hope. It may be that what you see is what you get, and both people and events are a common and steady lot. Days add upon days, tasks upon tasks, and the commonplace becomes the rule. We tell ourselves, "There needs to be more than this." Imagination responds.

Halloween may be the perfect festival. The mysterious is allowed full play, color and darkness blend in an unreal alliance, good and evil stage mock battles in which harm is an accident, and pretending becomes an acceptable way of life. Imagination allows us to escape banality and give existence an additional, exciting quality.

Halloween allows reality to hide behind masks of unreality. These are masks which none of us would accept as true, but which we should never grow too smart to wear.

❦ ❦ ❦

Few days are as intrinsically interesting as Thanksgiving Day. It is the celebration of a harvest and marks the end and rewards of labors which began with the melting snow so many months ago. It also is a celebration of the beginning of the holiday season and is filled with anticipation.

It may be the most significant and realistic of all our holidays. If it only recognized accomplishment, we would have little to spur us on; if it only initiated a renewed preparation for an oncoming season, we would be hesitant participants. But Thanksgiving is more. It is a time of rest and renewal; a day of garnering rewards and gathering promises.

This holiday is a human day giving full witness to achievement and expectation; to work and to hope. We are not satisfied with work done well, nor with aspirations alone. We would have both. The accomplishments of yesterday are best celebrated when they anticipate tomorrow. The fruits of our labors are most enjoyed when they are accompanied by the prospects of new possibilities.

Thanksgiving Day arrives with an announcement that we have done well and will do better.

❦ ❦ ❦

The season of Advent is a time of affirming that something good is going to happen, and it is going to happen to us. It arrives none to soon.

All year we have heard those who predict doom. They of course may prove to be correct, but what difference do they make to either the society around them or themselves? The people who make the changes, who move themselves and society, to whom monuments are raised, and whose names are praised, are those who expect good things to happen and do all within their power to make sure that they do.

If we don't expect good things to happen, it is almost certain that they won't. If, however, we expect the wonderful and prepare ourselves for it, there is a good chance that our expectations will be fulfilled.

Of course, we may be disappointed, but is that so bad? Isn't the expectation, in its own way, reward enough? It gave us some brightness for our days, and the disappointments can never take that away. To paraphrase Tennyson, "'Tis better to have expected and been disappointed, than never to have expected at all."

The Advent season initiates all the trappings of the Holidays, but most of all it brings a whisper which says to each and to all, "Expect, expect something good, something true, something wonderful to happen to you. Expect life."

❦ ❦ ❦

The celebration of Hanukkah, like many festivals of individual cultures, has its origin in military victory and violence. It commemorates the victory of Judah the Maccabee over the forces of Antiochus IV in 166 B.C.E. and as such

is part of a long series of armed successes and defeats
which have marked human history.

Surely the history of Hanukkah is remembered in many
families in its season, but the celebration has a lasting
place whether the origin is remembered or not. The lighting of the candles, the exchange of gifts, the games played,
and the special food all celebrate the Festival of Lights and
for most this is enough.

Perhaps this is the way it should be. The memories will
be guarded by institutions especially designed to do so—
and it is wise that this is so—but the people will find significance in the festival itself. It may be good that our deeds of war should finally evolve into an experience of
peace. The martial victory or defeat will be overwhelmed
by the ongoing march of history. A hundred or thousand
years from now it will not appear so vital, but the good
times will find renewed significance with every generation.

The wars of our era have scared us all. We would hate to
think that others will forget the pain, death and sacrifice.
But if in some dim future time, our hard days can become
an excuse for children's games, the real victory will have
been achieved. Peace, finally, is not the commemoration of
a victory, but a life of free laughter.

🦂 🦂 🦂

One of the central symbols of the Hanukkah and Christmas celebrations is the candle. Hanukkah candles filling
the holiday's menorah are a common sight in millions of
Jewish homes, and the lighting of these candles has become firm in the memory of Jews throughout the world.
Christmas candles, especially those which are included in

the annual "candles and carols" festivals, are so popular that they compete with pictures of Christmas trees and Santa Claus as proper representatives of the holiday.

It is fire that makes the candle so noticeable. Fire was one of humanity's earliest discoveries, and the one which may have been most vital in separating our forebears from their fellow creatures. With fire we have built and destroyed, created and eliminated, molded and ravaged.

Fire is the emblem of our achievements and the mark of our degradation. We gather around fire in these seasons because it represents the vitality of life itself. Hanukkah is more than a memory; Christmas is more than an ancient birth. The menorah reminds us of more than dreydls and chocolate coins; services of carols and candles are more than sentimental excursions into a vague nostalgia. It is the fire, not the beauty of the candelabra or the grace of molded wax, which marks the seasons. Fire with its fear and promise, fire with its power and mystery, fire with its beauty and adventure, calls each of us to realize the vitality of these amazing days and tales. No lesser symbol would have been fearful and wonderful enough.

❧   ❧   ❧

Families each Christmas are involved in one of the year's most difficult tasks: they are deciding who will remain on, and who will be removed from the Christmas card list.

We would like to think that the elimination of names from our lists is a confirmation of our firm grip on reality and a step towards financial responsibility. But if this were so, why is it so hard to erase the names? Why do we play games like, "Did they send us one last year?" Why do families argue over who stays and who goes, and why are the decisions so difficult?

We know why. We realize that those names on the list, including the people we haven't seen for years, and even those who haven't sent us a card in a decade, were once an essential part of our lives. We invested time, energy and ourselves into a relationship which we hesitate to dismiss. These were the people who stood by our sides in moments of sorrow or celebration, who heard our confessions and our exaltations, and who yesterday helped form today. To mark a line through their name is to pretend that we have forgotten, and we know we haven't.

The Christmas card list may be a nuisance, especially when there are so many other demands upon our time and energy, but it's not to be taken lightly. There is more here than a list. This is the honor roll of our lives. No wonder it's so difficult to remove names.

❦   ❦   ❦

For generations, Scrooge has been identified as the counter-hero of the Christmas season. His very name has become a symbol for greed and meanness. This argues that we still do not understand Dickens's story.

Scrooge is the hero of *A Christmas Carol*. Bob Cratchit is obsessed with survival and essentially invisible. Mrs. Cratchit is such a dutiful wife that we know her lines before she says them. And Tiny Tim is uniquely qualified to encourage little more than tears. But Scrooge, ah, there's a meat and potatoes character! He hates, he confesses, he complains, he repents, he laughs, and he weeps. There's real life in the old man.

And he changes, which is the heart of the story. The

other characters continue their established ways, but Scrooge is transformed. From the heartless employer, he becomes the generous friend. Out of the empty life, a person of promise arises. He gives notice that the holiday is more than sentimental excursions into a Never Never Land of flying reindeer and dancing elves, and more than merry greetings and pleasant family gatherings. Scrooge is Christmas at its roots.

It's not Santa Claus in children's dreams, but Scrooge arising from his dreams, who reveals the significance of the season.

❦   ❦   ❦

There will be a woman kneeling in everyone's creche this year, and we ought to know that woman. She kneels there and, for all practical purposes, is almost a stranger to all except the most devout Christians. That's too bad.

More than any other, she is the "Mother Idea" of civilization. She is the mother for whom all have searched and few, if any, have found. She is the mother inside every mother, and the mother to which we all cry in distress. She is to each of us, regardless of theological persuasion or cultural bias, the one who is universally recognized as "Mama." She is the one who, as Tova Reich noted in a *New York Times* article: "...in spite of all the evidence of the contrary, still insists, still knows, that we are good."

In this season, the usual question is: What child is this? That may not be the right question.

The days of Christmas are upon us, and the first person to arrive is a woman. What woman is this? She is a woman of comfort in the midst of a demanding and ultimately just world. What woman is this? She is the Mother to teach us wisdom and teach us love. She is Mary.

❦   ❦   ❦

It is not unusual for a child to refer to the gifts the three wise men brought to the Christ Child in the traditional Nativity story as: "Gold, frankincense, and *mirth*." Were that such were true!

One can't help wondering what kind of world ours might have become if mirth were one of the gifts which the rich and mighty brought to the crib of a holy child. How different our history would have been if one of the wise men had put on a funny hat and danced a jig. It could not help but be an improvement over myrrh which, even after all these centuries, still raises the question: "What?" Even when we know that it's a kind of perfume or incense, we aren't impressed. Mirth would have been better.

The holiday season is often a bore because we must spend so much energy being serious. It is claimed that Christmas is a time of joy. Really? Try assessing the truth of that by examining the schedules we keep.

The three wise men came bearing their gifts of gold, frankincense and myrrh. It probably seemed like a good idea at the time. But if it could be done over again, a little mirth would help.

❦   ❦   ❦

"Happy New Year!" How easily the words slip from our lips. The common salutation of the season rarely demands a second thought from either the one who speaks or the one who is spoken to.

What are we saying? Is this only a benign salute which has no interest beyond its being one of the accustomed pleasantries of polite society? Probably. At least, that is what we assume when we make such a glib exchange.

But "Happy New Year!" is a private wish made public. "I wish you a happy New Year," is a more complete statement of our intent. Our words convey the hope that our friends will be embraced by the blessings and rewards of the new year.

"Happy New Year!" is also our promise. We hereby pledge that we will not allow our ambition or pride to interfere with others' quest for happiness. Beyond that and wherever possible, we will offer our assistance in their quest.

"Happy New Year!" is a greeting, a wish, and a promise. Understanding these offerings, we may conclude that a simple nod of recognition is all the greeting that we choose to extend in this season. But then who would bid us, "Happy New Year!" and are we secure or arrogant enough to believe that we could live without it?

❦   ❦   ❦

No one celebrates the "Thirteenth Day of Christmas," and that's a relief.

This is a day for "getting on with the ordinary." If the traditional story were to continue, it would tell of how the Magi packed their festival clothes, put on travelling sandals, stuck a few souvenirs from Bethlehem into the corners of their saddle bags, and began the journey home. The shepherds would once again gather out under the night sky and view the ordinary and amazing heavens with which they were so intimately acquainted. Mary and Joseph would be the simple parents of a child who appears common enough to others, and a wonder to them. There is nothing unusual about that.

For our part, it's back to school or the workaday world. An occasional pine needle on the floor or candle wax on a dining room chair will remind us of the season that was, but the ordinary now abides. There is no cause for celebration here.

Nor is there cause for complaint. The ordinary, the familiar, and the routine have returned. They return, along with others, the common and the comfortable, and that is festival enough.

❧   ❧   ❧

Once again the time of hearts is here. Hearts mounted on boxes of presents, cakes molded into hearts, candies and boxes of candies shaped like hearts, paper hearts planted among gifts of flowers, and, of course, the multiple cards which have come to signify the season. Valentine's Day is here again.

The wisdom and grace to celebrate love, even puppy love, is a high mark of our civilization. The festivals of religious origins and commitments are simple enough to understand, the remembrance of great battles won are required excuses for holidays, and the birthdays of the famous and mighty will be noted with appropriate jubilees. This holiday, however, does something truly different. It is a special day to fête love. The human race has long taught the value of love and here is a day to honor it.

Valentine's Day needs no proclamation from politicians,

no memory of victory, and no honored host. It exists for the lovers of the world, most of whom will be ignored by all except those who receive their attention. The day is not in memory of the famous, but is a celebration of the tenderness, the caring, and the benevolent passion which make it all worthwhile.

If this love has not graced every life, then let the day honor those so adored. In time, each of us learns that love anywhere is a blessing to all everywhere.

❧   ❧   ❧

Ash Wednesday is not a popular religious festival. It shouldn't be. After all, Ash Wednesday's essential purpose is to recognize human mortality. For its part, mortality is simply a gentle word which translates into the realization that each of us will die and be forgotten. Hardly a day to celebrate.

Celebrate, no; remember, yes. Mortality is what we all have in common. We who differ in so many ways will all die. This is the ultimate democratic principle. The great and the ignored, the brilliant and the simple, those who live in mansions and the homeless, all meet as equals in this final reality. Like it or not, Ash Wednesday is real.

It is worthwhile to note that when the priest takes the ashes made from the once festive palm fronds and places them on the forehead of the faithful, the bearer cannot see the mark. He or she can only see the marks of mortality on others. Their mortality becomes obvious.

We need not see our own mark. We cannot live without others. They will die, and we will die. They will suffer, and we will suffer. We live in and through them, and they are mortal. Here, then, is Ash Wednesday's lesson: we are all in this together; no one is exempt; why, then, should we be deliverers of harm or the messengers of hate?

❧   ❧   ❧

The important thing about Ramadan, the holy month of Islam, is not the fast. Fasting serves only to remind.

Certainly the dawn-to-sunset fast is the most recognized element of Ramadan, but it is a mistake to think that devoted Muslims do not eat or drink during the daylight hours of this holy time because they hold to some kind of superstition. To fast and not recognize that the fasting is a reminder to do something is to miss the whole point of the discipline. Hunger is only a reminder, and a relentless one, that there is a task to be performed.

The task is self-examination, and it is a holy task. To reflect upon one's value system, the relations with neighbors, creatures and earth, what deeds are performed and what ignored; indeed, how one's life is being spent, is the core of Ramadan. This should not be difficult for non-Muslims to understand, for self-examination is also the core of Lent and Yom Kippur.

To be hungry during Ramadan is to be reminded that there is more, much more, to life than food.

❧   ❧   ❧

Palm Sunday, in addition to its historical and theological qualities, declares a time for cheering. This day recognizes that after the winter, the drudgery, the losses, and the disappointments, we need a victory, a chance to cheer about something. For some, it is a crocus blooming in spite of snow, or a chance to break the monotony of daily routine.

For others, it is an event which initiates pride in one's family, community or nation. For still others, it is a victory, perhaps a very minor one, which provides a ray of hope or a sense of significance. In any case, there is an occasion for excitement, light for dimmed eyes, and a time of cheering.

How dull and exhausting existence would be if there were no cheers. If there were no Palm Sundays in our lives, the Good Fridays would be unbearable, and Easter would be without meaning. We need something to cheer about, something to make our hearts beat a little faster, something which lifts us from the hollows which seem so often to be an everyday occurrence. It may be a birthday, a decent grade in school, a particularly good meal, or the completion of a much delayed task. Whatever, it calls for a cheer. We need to cheer; we need to hear cheers.

If Palm Sunday didn't exist, it would be necessary to create it. All of us deserve an event which is so thrilling and so fulfilling that we say: This is great; I'm enjoying myself; I like it!

❦   ❦   ❦

According to the Gospel writers, Jesus of Nazareth had been crucified, his body laid in the tomb, and the disciples had started a process of re-ordering their lives, when a few women knocked on the door and said (more or less): "Have we got a surprise for you!"

It is not too far afield to suggest that "surprise" is one of the lasting messages of Easter. Devout Christians find a continuing surprise in the ancient story of the empty tomb in the Palestinian hills. Those who find the winter too long rejoice in the surprising cycle of nature which displaces snow with budding flowers and introduces a robin before one was expected. Chroniclers note the surprises which are evident in the human venture, the whims of our allegiances, and the waywardness of this supposedly ordered society and planet.

Easter teaches us that life is not as finished, is not as predictable, and is not as dull, as we often believe. And how boring our lives would be if the unexpected disappeared.

We need structure, our sanity depends upon considerable security, and the proper management of our days requires an orderly universe, but we do not require a predictability which gives rise to tedium. Life is not, and must not be, exhausted by our experiences, our observations, or our learned forecasts. No good is finally ultimate. No evil is finally conclusive.

Ahead, just around the corner, unseen and unnoticed, lurks everyone's Easter. When least expected, it jumps from the shadows and says, "Have I got a surprise for you!"

❦   ❦   ❦

The cemetery monument is crumbling, but one can still read enough of the faded epitaph to know that it recognized a son's love for his mother and praised him for "faithfulness and filial affection."

The years have dimmed the message, but it still carries the emotion of that earlier time. Decades have passed, but the message has lost none of its poignancy. Much has changed since that stone was erected, the community is vastly different, and no one now living knew the man or his mother. The innocence of his age has been lost, and sentiment has almost dropped from our lives, but the words "faithfulness and filial affection," remain alive and true.

Mother's Day is often criticized in our sophisticated society. The day, however, retains its popularity, not through commercial excess as the cynics would have us believe, but because it represents an attitude and commitment which each of us, in better moments, recognizes. Deep down, where cynicism cannot reach, there remains an allegiance to values we hold dear. They are articulated in Mother's Day and, with or without prominent memories of a mother, the day calls us to honor "faithfulness and filial affection."

These words, and the day, remind us of something which we almost forgot....but didn't.

❦   ❦   ❦

The family gathered on the front porch. The chairs were arranged in order that the kin and visiting friends might watch the cars as they drove by on this, the only road which led to the cemetery. It was Memorial Day, and such was the tradition.

The cars passed at a steady rate all morning. Through the window of each, one could see flowers which would soon grace a grave on this Decoration Day. Most of the drivers and passengers were not aware of the little group sitting under the roof's shade, but others knew that the assembly would be waiting and waved as they drove by. "There go the Baxters," someone would say, and for a few minutes the conversation would turn to that particular family, and the memories which were provided. "There go the Anthonys," another would notice, and all would be reminded of the loss that the family faced only a short time ago.

It was a ritual of memory and community. The past was remembered and the present was acknowledged during this simple parade. When there was a break in the traffic, one might be tempted to reflect on some future Memorial Day when the porch would be empty or filled with strangers. The melancholy, however, was tempered by all in attendance for they were aware of the moment. It was a moment of remembering and renewing; of affirming a community with a beloved past and a hopeful future. We are always connected: sometimes with a wave from a friend; at other times with a bouquet of flowers.

For everything, and everyone, there is a season.

TO REPAIR THE WORLD

X

If the world must be repaired

—and it must—

we are the menders and furbishers.

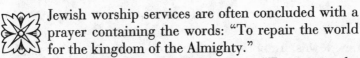 Jewish worship services are often concluded with a prayer containing the words: "To repair the world for the kingdom of the Almighty."

What a fascinating concept that is: "To repair the world." If we would allow our imaginations to soar and accept the creation story in Genesis for what it is—a magnificent metaphor providing hidden truths which we will still be discovering a thousand years from now—then one can visualize a very good, but not perfect, world at the beginning of time. One can assume that since it was not a perfect creation it has always been in need of repair.

It requires little insight to understand that, if the world needs repairing, human beings are the ones to do it. We may not be the most gifted creatures in the universe, but we are available. If the world must be repaired—and it must—we are the menders and furbishers.

It is evident that we live in a world of patches, wired parts, and poorly assembled pieces. It is obvious that those who were commissioned to do the repairing often didn't know what they were doing, but they could not deny the responsibility. Ours is a planet of mismatched parts, broken rivets, and crooked seams. Still, if the gods should return and visit their aging creation, we shouldn't be surprised if they are astounded by its beauty. After all, we who repair are minor creators and, to be fair, we are artists.

❦ ❦ ❦

One of the most difficult facts to incorporate in our understanding of life is the universal proposition that everything is temporary. The graspings of eternity are all about us. We build structures, write books, play music, and even implore the supernatural in attempts to partake in eternity.

Yet, all life argues that the only permanence is our knowledge that there is no permanence. Old towns die and new towns are born. Buildings are destroyed and replaced, styles change, people move, institutions are born, flourish and die. As the old words read, "Ashes to ashes and dust to dust"; finally, nothing remains.

This can give rise to a burdensome pessimism leading us to claim that "all is vanity," or we can learn to celebrate the temporary. After all, there is nothing wrong with temporality. Because a poem may not last throughout the ages is no reason to ignore it. Because a building will not stand forever is no reason to condemn it. To notice the fleeting beauty of a flower, or find the right apartment, or enjoy a moment of uproarious laughter are all values in good standing.

Our words may not live eternally, and our efforts may prove less durable than we planned, but does that really make any difference? If we could make the present moment sing and fill the passing sight with beauty, wouldn't that be enough?

❦   ❦   ❦

It is popular to claim that we are inheritors of this land and have a duty to protect and save this precious legacy. Few would question the intention and ethical awareness of this statement. But it's not true.

Inheritance implies ownership, and we don't own anything. We are simply passing through.

"This is mine" and "That is yours" are statements reflecting the practical aspects of living, but they have little to do with the ongoing reality. Nothing is finally ours. We are guests using whatever resources we can garner for our brief moment of survival in a universe which tolerates our visit. Ours is an existence of a traveler who clears and follows trails, and whose presence is a swift passing between two eternal unknowns.

We are guests with limited reservations, and our encounters will be remembered but briefly and then only if our lives are remarkable for their blessings or their banes. How foolish, therefore, to spend our scarce moments in enmity.

We own nothing, we inherit nothing, we are passing through and our behavior as guests is the judgment of our lives. It, therefore, would be appreciated if we did not pillage the resources, desecrate the altars, profane the language, insult the natives, or steal the towels.

❧   ❧   ❧

Most people, especially those in the traditional Western world, understand Ramadan, the holy month of Islam, as a demanding and restrictive time. Few, including devout Muslims, would challenge this. However, it may be that we will obtain a fairer appreciation for Islam, and many of the world's religious and secular disciplines, if we examine the exemptions as eagerly as we criticize its restraints.

The rules of Ramadan provide for the distinctive situations of women, the ill and travelers. The person who has special responsibilities, needs, limitations, or requirements is allowed considerable latitude in making adjustments to the mandates of this holy month. While the sacred days are not to be ignored, the observance must not cause harm or place unusual hardship on particular Muslims.

We might wish that our secular world be as generous. Few have escaped the unyielding decree: "It's against policy, there are no exceptions!"

When we want to know the truth about a community or a religion, it is important to know the rules and commandments, but a more thoughtful insight will be gained by understanding who is exempt and why.

At the end of the nineteenth century, Carl Schurz, then a Senator from Missouri, quoted the phrase Stephen Decatur coined ninety years earlier: "Our country right or wrong...." The Senator added: "When right, to be kept right; when wrong, to be put right."

The first phrase, when uttered without the second, is an unmitigated example of narrow nationalism. When the comments are joined, however, the statement becomes one of mature patriotism worthy of thoughtful and courageous citizens of all nations.

The sorrow is that here, as in so many cases, we listen to only part of the truth. It must be acknowledged that life is easier that way. We cannot deny the convenience of mouthing some simplistic view of nation, family or ourselves. "Our country, right or wrong," "My family, right or wrong," or "Myself, right or wrong," can be an excuse for every stupidity and asserted by the scoundrel or the hypocrite with abandon. It is the remainder of Schurz's statement, "When right, to be kept right; when wrong, to be put right," which exacts responsible reflection and unfailing effort.

Love for nation, neighbor, family or self requires more than an announcement. It requires the labor of mind and hand.

Everyone is a teacher, and all of us are constantly teaching. A few are selected by society to perform this task professionally, as part of a well-programmed activity with carefully assigned participants. The more informal and the more permanent teaching, however, is done by each of us all the time and everywhere.

Do not argue that we were never trained for such responsibility. Our whole life has been training us. All that have come within our sphere of influence are our teachers. We learned what they taught, and we learned how they taught. In our haste, we may forget our teaching role, but it is certain that others will not. Every time we meet, we teach.

The phrase, "How much I have learned from you!" is one of life's highest compliments. When we are filled with life's wonders, and when we are stripped by life's disappointments, we teach. When we are enthusiastic and quick, and when we are exhausted and foolish, we teach. When we are vital with health, and when we are consumed by pain, we teach. We were born to teach, and when we are dying we will be revealing silent secrets to those who are near.

We are all teachers, and it is an awesome responsibility. Paradoxically, we are all students, and that is even more awesome. It is a sobering fact to realize that the teachers we are can only teach what the students we are have learned.

❦   ❦   ❦

There are few words as troubling as the common word "generosity." It has the rare quality of something which we admire, yet fear to embrace. We recognize it as a virtue, and wonder if it is not naïve and perhaps stupid. We want others to be generous with us, but we have grave doubts whether or not we ought to be generous with them. Most of us recognize that generosity is essential for a worthy life, but we are not sure how or even why.

Perhaps it would be well for us to reconsider the word. For too long, it has been interpreted to mean giving others what they want. That may be foolishness. We might understand generosity as the act of sharing out of our bounty what others need. The verb to share rather than the verb to give is the key to understanding generosity.

Few enjoy such a bounty that they can afford to give much, but nearly all have enough to share. It is in that sharing that we learn to become responsible agents of generosity, rather than gullible victims of the crafty. Once we learn the difference between giving and sharing, we find generosity far less troubling. Our sharing will help us to realize how prosperous we are. With this understanding and sufficient generosity, we will become rich.

❦   ❦   ❦

Alienation has joined us on our travels because our age issued the invitation. When survival was our all-consuming task, alienation was unknown. With the coming of affluence—and our age, burdened as it is with inflation and recession, is still extraordinarily affluent—comes an awareness of both leisure and alienation.

The answer to this situation is to "do something." But relief arrives only when we "do something that matters." Our days are full of work, most of which is vital for our continuing existence, but what do we do that matters? There is no limit to our efforts—most of us are exhaust-ingly busy—but we fail in directing our efforts towards something that is truly worthwhile. As long as we live our lives involved in filling time with "something to do," we will know alienation. Only when we "do something that matters" will our emptiness and separation cease.

When we recognize a world beyond ourselves and care about it, when we view our leisure as a time for something rather than a time for nothing, when we remember that self-discipline is the prerequisite to maturity, and when we choose greatness rather then fashion, then will we do something that matters and find an answer to alienation. Empty days will be filled when we fill them with the abundantly available needs and hopes. When that happens, alienation will return to whatever dank corner it used to call home.

❦ ❦ ❦

There is bad news. The world is not coming to an end! Armageddon is not going to arrive, and we are going to continue our lives, generation after generation, in an ongoing world.

There is a romantic quality to the concept of Armageddon. Most of us recognize how thrilling it would be to live in the last age. There is a dark romance in visualizing flying missiles and exploding bombs. The romantic escapism of rolling clouds and buckling earth has its own strange and frightening set of temptations.

We who live and will continue to live on this less exciting planet will find romance, but not the exciting romance of the end of time. We are going to live in the workaday world which we have come to know so well. There will be mouths to feed, poverty to be eliminated, corruption to be eradicated, peace to be promoted, the ignorant to be educated, and diseases to be cured. There is little romance here.

Such mundane tasks do erect barriers against the tiny Armageddons which attack this planet. To feed the hungry, house the homeless, enlighten the dull, provide hope for the despairing, and love one another, is a worthy romance.

❦　❦　❦

Problems are tricky. They often seem to be contagious and, unless we are careful, they "travel" to others without reducing the pain of the original host. To put it another way, problems feign a quality like measles and are "passed" from one person to another without relieving the illness of the original carrier.

If we wish to partake in the process of solving problems, it will be necessary for us first to understand just who has the problem. To confuse this situation, or to assume that we have a problem when that is not the case, or to believe that we can relieve another's suffering by acquiring it ourself, is to make the potential solution formidable, if not impossible.

We cannot solve problems which are not ours to solve, and others cannot solve our problems. While there is little doubt that we would gladly assume the problems which plague our friends and family if that would relieve them of pain, it cannot be done. While we would often like to transfer our difficulties to others, it cannot be done.

As long as there are people on this planet there will be problems. It is our hope that many of these problems will be eliminated or reduced. But it is certain that none of these will be relieved until we understand who has the problem.

❧   ❧   ❧

The great Hindu philosopher Radhakrishnan once wrote: "Those who light a little candle in the darkness will help to make the whole sky aflame."

This truth, so basic to Hinduism and so vital for all of us, gives poetic witness to an evasive fact: We often forget that our little efforts of support and our little acts of goodwill make a difference. We are so mesmerized by the actions of the powerful and the enterprises of the famous, we fail to apply our single wills and ways to the problems of existence. Convinced that we cannot do something grand, we elect to do nothing at all. What a pity! The darkness we could dispel continues, and the lights of the world are dimmed.

Radhakrishnan speaks to us. He draws our attention to an awareness that the sky becomes aflame slowly. The growth of good is not some solitary, magnificent act which envelopes the world in a blinding flash. It is the steady, slow development of one light added to another. These lights, these good deeds, by themselves appear to be insignificant and unworthy of notice. Yet when they are added to others, the brighter light grows, and it illuminates the world.

We are an impatient lot, waiting and expecting an immediate and splendorous occurrence to mark our lives and our times. Still, most of us will learn, sooner or later, that growth is slow, but it increases; that our deeds are frail, but not insignificant. Occasionally, the good and wise glance at the sky and they see the spreading light—the light of their own creation.

❦   ❦   ❦

"There are some things a man just has to do." It sounds like a line out of a movie Western, and it is. The statement, usually said to a wife or girlfriend while the man straps on his pistols in preparation to meet the foe, is a common expression of movieland valor and morality.

Yet this is more than some scriptwriter's cliché. Change the phrase to "There are some things a person just has to do," and the words speak directly to us all. Here we find the core of commitment to personal morality. It is always the "things we have to do," which mark the state of our moral consciousness.

To say, "There is nothing I have to do," confesses more than planned. The one who believes that social and political liberties sweep away the demands for personal commitments betrays the ultimate goal of public freedom: The personal moral code. Liberty is the framework for individual ethics, not a license for moral anarchy.

Contrary to popular slogans, morality can be legislated, but such legislation pales beside the moral actions initiated by the individual conscience. The person who acts against injustice because of allegiance to justice, who stands for the downtrodden because of loyalty to the human community, and who pledges him or herself to reduce hatred because of commitment to love, is both the first and strongest line of defense against barbarity.

"There are some things a person just has to do." Thank goodness.

❦   ❦   ❦

Compassion is a disorderly value, but it is a value. Unlike justice, it does not enjoy the acclaim of literature, no profession is garnered and trained for its support, and few temples are raised in its name. Yet compassion is always with us, like a beggar soliciting on the Court House steps, or a saint sitting silently in a back pew. Compassion keeps reminding us that justice is essential, but it is not all.

The person who makes the just decision is acclaimed, as he or she should be. In this world filled with knaves and charlatans, we desperately need men and women who will act justly. Who among us doesn't bare scars from injustice? But the compassionate person, who by the very fact of a compassionate act, must twist the just decision, rarely receives acclaim. Compassion must be its own reward, for it will rarely be rewarded by others.

In this world where justice is such a fleeting item, where injustice still runs rampant in all cultures, there is longing for the just society and the just person. It will be a magnificent day when there is "justice for the lot of each." But with that justice, we might also hope for compassion. Without it, the "judgment which runs down as waters" will become as ice, and the ancient prophecy chill the world.

❦   ❦   ❦

Few of us are willing to be unprepared for the future. In a variety of ways, we seek to equip ourselves for whatever awaits around the corner of our lives. We set aside funds for a rainy day, build a nest egg against that time when ordinary resources are unavailable, purchase insurance, establish pension programs and propose alternatives should our normal procedures be obstructed. Such action is considered wise, and those who oppose it would be judged foolish.

Yet, anticipation carries its own danger. To anticipate is to predict and, unless care is maintained, anticipation dictates the form and nature of our reaction. When this happens we may be unprepared for sudden or subtle changes. For example, we can form an opinion of a child, anticipate a child's misbehavior, create an environment in which the predicted may occur, and prepare our automatic response. Given such an environment, the child is almost certain to meet expectations.

Our sense of responsibility and survival demands that we anticipate the future. This insight, however, needs to be balanced against the reality of changes. Things may not be as we expect, and our ability to adapt is as important as our ability to anticipate.

Wisdom resides in those who combine careful analysis with cautious responses, the steady eye with the quick mind, and the clenched fist with the listening ear.

❦   ❦   ❦

It was an interesting class assignment: Name the five most detrimental problems in our society. The difficulties were the expected ones: Poverty, racism, war, sexism, economic imbalance, crime, etc.

The next day's assignment was equally interesting: Name the causes of these problems. When the lists were compiled they contained the anticipated villains: Politics, institutions, corporations, capitalism, collectivism, etc.

It is fascinating to note that not one member of the class listed himself, herself or a neighbor as a cause of society's problems. Yet who among us can doubt, especially in those

moments of severe honesty, that he or she hasn't contributed a goodly share to the general difficulties of the world.

This is not to fall back on the old escape clause which
argues if everyone is guilty, then no one is guilty. It is not
to ignore the evils encouraged by the institutions, structures and elites. But the first step towards providing a society which is beneficial to its people and supportive of its
citizens is always a thorough examination of ourselves. Unless we can see in ourselves the racism, hatred, prejudice
and greed that plague our communities, there is little reason to assume that any improvements in the social structure are imminent.

It would be nice to wake up tomorrow morning and find
reformed institutions battling the myriad evils of this
planet. This is unlikely, for the simple reason that not
enough of us woke up this morning battling the evils
within ourselves.

❦   ❦   ❦

Good deeds aren't worth much unless they are accompanied by good times. The bored solicitor isn't going to raise
much money, the perfunctory board member is usually bereft of ideas, and the tepid tutor does little to inspire his
pupil.

Good deeds have bad reputations. Do-gooders are often
portrayed as some "Simple Sam" or "Plain Jane" characters who lead dull lives and, probably, aren't very bright.
It's high time to be done with such caricatures. Where our
good deeds are boring, they should be revived by breathing
fresh air into them; where our noble actions have become
monotonous, let us throw out the old procedures and in-
stall those methods which give us a sense of joy and ac-

complishment; where needed tasks have become dull routines, let us rekindle the original sense of caring and blend it with our own commitment to the worthwhile life.

The good deed should not only bring a smile to one's conscience, but also a smile to one's face; it should not only bring joy to others, but also joy to us. The good deed should not only make us feel better about others, but also feel better about ourselves and with others. The success of the good deed is not simply dependent upon good actions, but upon good environment. Good deeds and good times are truly inseparable.

ॐ   ॐ   ॐ

Everyone, sooner or later, repeats with a sigh the old words, "We did what we thought was right at the time." This statement attempts to convey that, given what information and intuition was available, we tried to do the right thing. The sincerity of our defense is not denied.

Yet the words are uttered with a sigh because the results did not meet expectations. It seemed, at the time, that this was the required action, but we failed. It should have been the right thing to do, but it wasn't. The sigh also could suggest some new factor has been revealed which changes everything. A new detail may have become known, or an unexpected development has altered our efforts. Whatever, we would not have done what we did, had we known. "We did what we thought was right at the time," becomes a statement of defeat simply because we did not know everything.

Such an admission of defeat is unworthy of us. We need not be ashamed of our actions. To do what is correct in the light of available information is one of our finest acts. If hidden factors arrive, if new information is later revealed, it doesn't change the clear and noble fact that our original performance was the best we could have offered. We should be proud that we did what was right in response to the times. Such action is rare in our society and age, and it should be honored.

To do what we thought was right at the time is all that can be asked of any of us. If it later proves to be ineffective or mistaken, nothing has been lost from the original attempt. It forever remains right and good.

❦ ❦ ❦

Inspirational addresses are not hard to recognize, and they too often have the single quality of being easily forgotten. Who, for example, can remember those words which seemed so stirring when we graduated from high school or college? Being moved and not being able to remember what it was that moved us is not an unusual failing.

Yet there was one sentence from a commencement address, delivered more than a century ago, which still haunts those who read it, as it must have troubled those young people in Antioch College who heard it for the first time in 1859. The speaker was Horace Mann, and his words were: "Be ashamed to die until you have won some victory for humanity."

Such words, delivered near the eve of the Civil War, must have seemed terribly ironic for those young men who were to die before the first victorious battle. One wonders if they were ashamed, or was the very fact that they were participating in a cause which seemed worthwhile a kind of victory, no matter what the outcome of a particular engagement?

But will we be ashamed? Mann's words remain vital not simply because they challenge, but because they force us to act within the context of our mortality. It is not simply a call to do some noble deed someday, but to be ashamed of ourselves if we do not act. The words live afresh with each generation because they do not allow an escape.

True inspiration does not make us feel comfortable with the speaker. It makes us feel uncomfortable with ourselves.

❦   ❦   ❦

The man stood alone on the sidewalk. He was about fifty years of age, obviously poor, dirty, disheveled, and was standing there with his hand out. One might have assumed he was a beggar, and many did as they sought to avoid his plea. Yet, when we paid attention, it became apparent that he wasn't seeking money from those who were passing by—he wanted them to shake his hand. He wasn't seeking coins, he was seeking something much more demanding: He was seeking attention. Here on a busy street, a human being asked for recognition from his fellows. It was rarely granted.

It is tempting to believe that, if the situation had been adequately explained, those who feared his request for money would have granted his request for a handshake. But would they? Would we? After all, he was not one of us, he could not have been recognized by our crowd, he had few of the symbols which define those with whom we readily shake hands. He was a stranger.

Or was he? How quickly might we become such a stranger? Is it possible that we might find ourselves cut off from the friendly grasp of the human and civilized community? How much of him is in us? How far removed are we from the desire to hear a friendly word or to feel a warm touch?

The stranger was not so strange. He needs what we need, longs for that for which we long, and, like us, learns to get by with what is offered. We are going to assume that he is crazy. We must. If he is not, we are forced to face a reality which may tell us more than we want to know.

❦   ❦   ❦

Scholars tell us that James Madison, the father of the United States Constitution, was a man totally devoid of charisma. He was not handsome, articulate, or charming. He, however, had one overwhelming asset: he was always prepared.

This is good news. Living in an age in which charisma is considered the most valuable of all gifts, the vast majority of us are found wanting. We will not be the winners of beauty contests, we find speaking before large audiences and in public debate both frightening and embarrassing, and charm was always offered by a school which ignored our applications. Charismatic, alas, we are not; but preparation is something else.

Preparation doesn't demand the chiseled features, the glib tongue or a captivating smile. It is available to all, and totally democratic. Preparation has a way of making its own impression, establishing the proper boundaries, and winning the day. Beauty, grace and urbanity are impressive, but preparation is immortal.

Heads may not turn when the prepared arrived, but minds will change. Few may weep or faint when the prepared speak, but their words endure. The smiles and handshakes of the prepared may be forgotten, but their

facts and efforts will be remembered. These are the rewards of preparation, and we are all eligible.

ROSES IN WINTER

XI

Snow may blanket every patch of former life, and our world seem sterile as glass, but our minds retreat from the onslaught of harsh reality and we dream of roses.

The study of history is not the best way to obtain an understanding of the future, it is the only way. This elementary knowledge is embarrassingly simple, yet we ignore it as if it were useless. There is no lack of attention directed to those who proclaim that they can foresee the future. Experts at forecasting, even those who are well recognized charlatans, never lack an audience. A noted historian, however, must earnestly labor to gather a meager crowd of listeners.

This is an interesting reflection on our time, and perhaps on all times. Each age wants to believe that it is prominent, critical, and unique. Our forebears could not possibly have experienced what we have experienced. They were not smart enough, sensitive enough, or powerful enough. This must be one of the great marks of our and every generation's arrogance: to believe that no one could have faced our problems; no one could have suffered as we have suffered.

But sooner or later we must acknowledge a truth: we walk backwards into the future, and all we can know is right there in front of us.

❦   ❦   ❦

Some time ago a historic church building in an eastern city burned to the ground. It was a great loss for the church's congregation and the community which loved the old structure.

A saddened assembly gathered the following Sunday to assess its loss and commit itself to the terribly expensive and backbreaking effort of rebuilding. Fortunately, the minister had both the insight and wisdom to renew the vitality of the people by proclaiming that, "We have lost our building, but not our church."

This declaration is a vital affirmation for all. We may, in any of myriad forms, lose our building, but not our church. We often are tempted to confuse buildings with processes, resulting in a confusion of values and a misunderstanding of goals.

There is no limit as to how much we may lose or how much is unaffected by the loss. We may lose our house, but not our home. Our children may leave our community, but the family remains. We may lose our respectability, and in doing so retain our self-respect. Our youthful appearance may dissolve, but life endures.

We need to learn the art of holding on easily. Much is going to be taken away, slip away, or be destroyed. We can let go. What holds on to us is far more important.

❧   ❧   ❧

The first question to be asked in meeting any difficulty is: Have we been through this before? History, whether it be social or personal, has as its vital purpose the retardation of repetition. If we have no memory of experiences, or if our memories are limited by our desire to evade or avoid attention, then history becomes little more than a chronicle of follies.

"What have we learned?" is a question which must be asked time after time, and it is a procedure which we surely will attempt to avoid. To seek an answer to such a question, and not to settle for the first ready reply which suits our immediate need or reduces criticism, is one of life's most agonizing tasks.

This is nothing short of probing the pain. Who wants to

do this? No one. Who must do this? All who are not willing to let truth lie hidden and unacknowledged, all who are not willing to let evil go unnamed, and all who believe that it is not necessary to repeat tragedies anew in every generation.

"What have we learned?" This is a simple question which accepts no simple answers. This is a searching question whose pursuits threaten to be painful. This is a hopeful question whose revelations may bring calm to a fretful mind and peace to a tortured world. If we have not learned to ask "What have we learned?", we may have learned nothing at all.

❦   ❦   ❦

We remember how slowly the years passed from the time we were twelve until we were eighteen. The years seemed to crawl by, and we yearned to be sixteen and then seventeen and finally eighteen. To youth, time is a laggard.

Not so with adults. A score of years is but yesterday, a decade hardly provides a chance to become acquainted, and those six years, which passed so sluggishly when we were teenagers, are but a few fleeting moments. For adults, the years do fly by.

It is tempting, therefore, to gaze with regret at the exited years. "What happened to all that time?" we wonder. Twenty years have lapsed, and what have we to show for them? What happened to the dreams, the hopes, the plans? "How," we ask ourselves, "did we waste so much time?"

The dreams may not have been realized, the ambitions may not have been achieved, and the only things we may have to prove the years we lived are our grown children and grey hair. But we were, in those years, a part of the great context of life. We gave and received, planted and harvested, taught and learned. We also gave to the future as we received from the past, planted crops whose fruit we will never see, harvested provender from the unknowable, learned lessons discovered by the ancients, and prepared paths for the unborn.

It is true that the years are fleeting, but we are participants in eternity.

🐝   🐝   🐝

Tradition has it that Martin Luther was once asked what he would do if he knew the world were to end tomorrow. He answered, "I would plant an apple tree today." Such is not simply a good answer. It's probably the only answer. Luther may have believed some things about that final day which we may or may not believe, but his attitude regarding the next-to-the-last day transcends belief. It portrays an understanding of life and how it is to be lived.

We may not receive notice of the final day, but that makes little difference. If we are living our lives to their full, the final days should look much like all the others. Each of us learns, sooner or later, that life cannot be treated like school studies in which one attempts to learn a semester's work two weeks before final examinations. We live each day as best we can, we contribute to our neighbors and ourselves, we build and plant for tomorrow.

What folly it would be to weep on the next-to-last day regretting all that we had missed, all that we had postponed. Better that such a day finds us planting apple trees, affirming what we have been, continuing to be what we are. The worthiness of life rarely arrives in some single moment of thrill or courage. It resides quietly in the chores, the plans, and the loves that are always near. Each of us has an apple tree to plant, and the planting makes the last day as glorious as the first.

❦   ❦   ❦

One of our most difficult tasks is to honor the past. Some would ignore the times gone by, claiming that they are nothing but a series of mistakes, while others ignore the past by asserting they only look to the future. Still others will idolize it, claiming that the former days hold all that was valid, and we are squandering our heritage.

Honoring the past, however, would best be done by neither disregarding nor deifying our yesterdays. We would honor the past best by using it. We offer our greatest respect, not by veneration, but by utilization. Our heritage, if it is worthy, offers us teachings and courage. Without these the present is meaningless, and the future is fearful.

One honors the past by contributing to the future. Our forebears brought us to this point in history by moving forward, not by standing still. It would be a disservice to them to reverse our journey. They had the courage to travel new roads in their time. Surely that courage inspires us to travel the unknown in our day. What praise would it be if we were to erect monuments to their work and fail to make such labor our own?

The past is the past. It can be an idea, a building or a person. Let us honor that past by expanding the idea, helping new life flow in old structures of mind and stone, and memorializing our heroes the only way they would want to be remembered: In living our lives with the courage they inspire in us.

We honor the past by remembering what was as we prepare what will be.

In one of Thomas Merton's poems, he refers to "A working horizon." Such a concept defines the boundaries and the goals of personal life, while remaining open for changes and potentials.

Isn't a "working horizon" what we all need? The horizon remains a point at which each of us judges growth and establishes aims. There are few things more frustrating than a horizon so distant that it negates our sense of accomplishment. Of what use is a goal so unattainable that it cannot be reflected in our day-to-day living? On the other hand, what reward is there in acknowledging a horizon which is only an easily conquered hill? If the goals of our lives do not test the quality of our endeavors, how do we judge our growth?

A "working horizon" is fundamental. It is distant enough to challenge us with a consistency which forbids our laziness or the acceptance of inferior ideals. It is near enough to supply sufficient rewards in order that we do not become bored with the impossible or incapacitated by a sense of failure.

The "working horizon" protects us from two great temptations: The temptation of insignificance and temptation of omnipotence. We should always be careful that our horizon or goal or God is neither too far nor too near.

It had been a stimulating lecture and, through the generosity of the speaker, he and a few members of the audience were discussing the topics of the day, when a young woman asked a question regarding a social issue and one of its spokesmen. "What your friend fails to understand," replied the learned lecturer, "is that he has won the battle, his enemies have surrendered, his friends have furled their battle flags, and the controversy is over; but he will not recognize it."

As it is true of other people and other issues, so it is true of us. There are times when we have accomplished what we set out to do, but we seem unwilling to recognize the finished fact. Trained as we are for battle, we find it difficult, if not impossible, to realize that the conflict is over and victory is ours. We continue to act and think as if the warfare is still raging and the enemies still threaten.

Perhaps we have a difficult time seeing ourselves as victors. So accustomed have we become to combat that we find no identity in triumph. As a result, we become pathetic figures who fight useless issues and bore our friends with outdated war stories.

Before we don our battle raiment again, it might be well for us to evaluate the level of hostilities. The conflict may be over. With our energies in so short supply, it is a shame to waste them contending with shadows.

❧   ❧   ❧

Saying hello is a natural and joyous experience, but we must learn to say good-bye. Those who would seek to live a whole life must, sooner or later, come to an awareness of the essential quality of saying good-bye. This good-bye is not to be confused with those ready remarks which we use to denote the temporary separation of friends or associates. This is the difficult good-bye which marks the end of a relationship.

There are many good-byes. The good-bye to friends who will become a brief address on Christmas card lists, the good-bye to enemies and hates which are products of old battles and tired memories, the good-byes to ideas and hopes which are no longer viable and where attempts at resurrection would only result in frustration. And, of course, there is the good-bye that comes with death which, although cherishing the memory, allows the necessary release for the new life.

Each of us can add to the list of good-byes: The conclusion of a period in history, the lapse of long-held beliefs, the searing experience of divorce, and others. These are the conscious good-byes in our lives from which no one is exempt.

Sooner or later, each of us, in his or her own way, learns that if we can't say good-bye, we will be unable to bid anyone hello. In a quiet and special way, the good-byes are essential to freedom.

❦   ❦   ❦

When we look at our lives, it is somewhat refreshing to note that what is happening to us is not happening for the first time in all creation. Others have faced the same problems we face, others have battled the same diseases we battle, others have found solutions to the difficulties which confuse us, others have looked at their world and have seen chaos, and these others have found that existence makes sense.

Sooner or later we come to realize that our problems are

not unique, and we don't have to re-invent the wheel. As we live, we come to understand that others have felt the pain we feel, have known the hurt we have experienced, and have sought solutions as we seek them. They found relief for the pain, reduction for the hurt, and relevant solutions. The wheel has been invented, and we don't have to do it again.

We are not the "first generation"; we are the "next generation", and as such we are inheritors. We have inherited good, old wheels. They work just fine. In many cases, we can't do any better. We can save much time, much effort, and much disappointment. There are old wheels we can use. We need not always be creators. That is what it means to be the "next generation," and it is wonderful.

❦   ❦   ❦

T. S. Eliot reminded us that ambition arrives "when early force is spent and no longer all things possible." Which, of course, is true. Ambition comes when we find need to protect ourselves, protect our interests, and protect that which protects us. The very core of ambition is the effort to obtain and maintain sufficient power that we may distance ourselves from that which threatens.

We often hide our ambition. It is easy to understand it as an intrinsic weakness which bodes no good. We may even try to pretend that it is not. However, ambition may not be one of our more attractive marks, but it is surely a mark of the mature.

Let us be ambitious for a better life for ourselves and all others. Let us be ambitious for our children, and others' children. Let us be ambitious for a more peaceful, more sane, more intelligent, more understanding, and more loving world. Let us be ambitious for the younger generation which, more than previous generations, may be creatively ambitious when their time inevitably arrives, and they realize that their "early force is spent."

🕯   🕯   🕯

Most of us live with the myth that everything can be finished. We labor to finish a project, bring a task to an end, and complete obligations. We like to think, "Well, that's over."

Yet, there are few items in this life which are finished, and much of our labor—especially the most vital —is never completed. The beds are made, but they will be rumpled in a few hours; the semester will end, but a new one will begin shortly; the business arrangement may be accomplished, but we will begin new negotiations tomorrow. There are few completions, and that is the way it should be.

We might yearn for our lives to be a series of "jobs completed," but this will never be. Living is a continuing line of activities and opportunities. We are always participating in a new project before the old one has been concluded. It is simply not the nature of life to stop. The situations of our lives will change, but life will go on. Indispensable concerns and goals will be expended, but we will survive. Old facts will give way to new insights, but truth will carry on. Sooner or later we learn that few small activities, and no large ones, are finished. Life, the ultimate activity, is never completed.

Life is a continuum and as such is inescapably immortal.

The Native American adage that you should not criticize another until you have walked a mile in his moccasins is sage advice. And it is equally true that good counsel is most likely to come from one who has walked a mile in the moccasins we are about to wear.

The best guidance most of us will ever know will be received from those who have been through what we are going through, or about to go through. The loss of objectivity when it comes to evaluating a situation which one knows well is surely balanced by hands-on experience. That another has gone through what we are about to go through gives a sense of authority which all can recognize.

Perhaps the greatest value of growing older is the simple fact that one has lived long enough to have gathered a real sense of experience. No longer dependent upon what others say, we can now speak for ourselves. The phrase "I did" speaks with far more authority than the phrases "I read" or "I thought."

❦ ❦ ❦

"What is, isn't all." We need to write that lesson indelibly in our minds. To forget it would be to negate the very essence of humanity.

We who are so impressed with our grasp of reality live with the constant temptation to say, "This is it." What we understand is not "it." There is always more.

A day does not pass when we fail to meet friends and neighbors who are not what they were. How unfortunate it would be if what we see is all of what they are. There was a time when they were the bright lights of their families, they were the sought-after laborers in the necessary vineyards, they were the hope of tomorrow. Should we fail to remember this, we participate in a sad injustice. All who come within our view are more than they now seem, and we know it.

Value is not a timebound thing. It is yesterday and tomorrow just as surely as it is today. If this were not so, who among us would be valued, who could be admired, and who would hold promise? "What is, isn't all," is an announcement of the history and the justice which finally rescues each of us.

🐛 🐛 🐛

The clouds which had been so heavy and dark were sliding towards the northeast and a bright blue sky was peeking through, when the young girl confidently announced, "It's all over." She then added, "It feels good to say that something is 'all over.'"

Indeed it does. One of the slogans we human beings cherish is "It's all over." We learn at an early age that we can tolerate almost anything if we can look forward to a time when one can say "It's all over." This phrase supplies a feeling of deep satisfaction and sometimes a sense of relief.

There are, of course, times when we do not want to say these words as they mark too much of an ending. We would postpone such conclusion, but that is impossible. The finite quality of all existence, whether it be a blessing or bane, is inescapable.

The sadness which is part of our finite character is inevitable, but the scales tip—sometimes weakly, sometimes mightily—in favor of benevolence. Endings often do contribute more than they deduct.

George Santayana is acclaimed for having written: "Those who cannot remember the past are condemned to repeat it." Few would deny the truth and insight of these words, but it is important to remember that Santayana's wisdom was directed to remembering the past, not dwelling upon it. The past is our best teacher. To ignore it, to forget it, to deny it is to be placed in immediate danger of not only repeating the past, but of repeating the worst part of it. Any event in our personal lives, or the history of the society, no matter how individually tragic or communally dreadful, stands a good chance of being repeated when we forget.

To dwell upon the past, however, carries evils of its own. How awful it is to witness either those forlorn souls or miserable societies who are obsessed with the past. When we are obsessed by the wrongs we have suffered or the losses we have known, when we can only dream of the glory that once was or the achievements our forebears claimed, our lives and the lives of our community shrink.

Surely the past must be remembered. In it we will find old joys, fond memories, and hard-won lessons. Let it, however, only be remembered, and then let us press forward to tomorrow where wrongs may be righted, losses redeemed, achievements claimed, and dreams made real. The past has memories and lessons; the future has promise and life. Remember the past; pursue the future.

ɞ ɞ ɞ

The good things of life come in a variety of ways, and not the least of these lies in the fact that the future is hidden. There are those who claim they want to know what tomorrow holds, but if such knowledge should become available, even at bargain rates, probably few would buy. If tomorrow's events would be revealed today, we might be tempted to turn and run. Most of us would rather meet life as it comes than to brood over the foreseeable.

If we examine our own histories, we may well find the stuff of personal inspiration. Who among us, when considering our yesterdays, doesn't say: "How did I manage to live through that?" We who have accumulated a few years have lived through times which, upon reflection, seem overwhelming. Yet, we made it. We survived simply because we didn't know what was coming and when it arrived we lived one day at a time until the crisis passed.

Here, therefore, is strength for all. We have been through difficult times before and endured. We can continue. Difficult times will come again and, thank goodness, we do know neither where nor when, but we will overcome or, at least, muddle through. Look at what we have already experienced!

When we are well acquainted with our past, there is little reason to fear our future. Those who are "over the hill" developed real strengths during the climb.

❦   ❦   ❦

No doubt there will be a time, twenty years from now, when someone will resurrect the music and fashions of these present times, and we will long for the good old days. They may look pretty good from that distance, but we who live here recognize the difficulties of these years. The crises, economic burdens, international chaos, and violence are matters not easily ignored, nor should they be. Yet it might be well to understand that our times may not be as bad as we might think. Perhaps these days are candidates for the good old days.

Certainly the evils and difficulties of our age cannot be denied. All wish their children lived in a kinder, cleaner world. We, however, recognize that the only hope for such improvement lies in a clear realization of the facts and lessons of these years.

No doubt, we have made mistakes and our greed has brought its full share of evil into our time. Let us not lose our sense of outrage, or relax our vigilance as we seek a clean, safe world. But let us recognize that there is much which is wonderful here.

We have problems, but they are less debilitating than those faced by our forebears. In fact, when we get down to it, these may be the "good old days." For us, of course, there's not much of an option.

❦   ❦   ❦

He is an unimportant man making an insignificant protest at an inconsequential location. Nothing will come of it.

Then why is his appearance so haunting?

It is more than an awareness that great changes sometimes arise out of such humble beginnings. Such developments are so rare as to be unworthy of our serious attention. No, there is something else here which disturbs us. It has something to do with the fulfillment which transcends success.

Doing what one believes must be done, even when it is clearly known that such action will produce nothing of significance, is beyond the moral grasp of most of us. We lesser types have no time for such impracticality. We want to know what good will come of what action, what important opinion will be changed, and what effect will be achieved. We want to make a difference; we want to accomplish something.

To watch this man practice his lonely vigil is to witness a rarity: A person who is freed from the tyranny of results.

❦   ❦   ❦

The last rose of summer is dead. We might pretend otherwise. We may purchase roses and imagine that they were freshly picked from our garden. We might place a silk rose on the mantle and suspend reality long enough to believe that it was growing outside our window a few minutes ago. A ceramic rose may grace our coffee table and, in the right light, seem almost real. But we know better.

Winter is here, and the roses are gone. The coatless days, the hot sun warming brown earth, the smells of flowers blooming in frenzy, the open windows providing a stage for dancing curtains, and green life growing against time, all belong to a season irrevocably past. It is winter now, and we bundle ourselves against grey skies and harsh winds. We will not suffer much. We know the darker season and are prepared. These skies and winds are not strangers and, with head bowed against the cold, we will struggle along as we have struggled before.

But the roses—how we will remember the roses! The bitter winds may whip around our homes, and their howl will tell us again and again of the bleak despair which has captured the roses, but recollection of what was still lingers. Snow may blanket every patch of former life, and our world seem sterile as glass, but our minds retreat from the onslaught of harsh reality and we dream of roses. We will not, cannot, and should not be satisfied with the bleak winter. Memories of our summers may bless us still.

When icy reality destroys the last rose, the memory of the summer's lush garden will ease the cold, and memory will prove more lasting than winter.

❦   ❦   ❦

There is nothing like a walk through a cemetery to give one's life perspective, and the older the cemetery the better.

To realize that people, not great people but common people like ourselves, lived full lives and died decades, and even centuries before we were born carries a message of lasting reality. It is one thing to read about notable lives in history books or enjoy the imaginations of gifted writers and actors on movie and television screens. It is quite another thing to amble through a cemetery and read the names and dates of people who are now gone and come to understand that they, too, once loved life. They saw what we see, they walked these grounds, grieved at these very graves, and died long before the momentous events of our age—by which we assess the value of our lives—occurred.

Did they, we might wonder, think they were living in exciting times? Did they believe that the world was on its last legs, or that the younger generation was irresponsible? Were their pains and heartaches worse than ours, their happiness better?

Someday the curious will look upon some mark of our existence and, undoubtedly, wonder as we wonder now. We might tell them that their thoughts are not new, that their machines, conveniences and styles differ from ours, but not much else. We might convey that we had their questions, their doubts, their hopes. We might give them our answers, but let's not. Why spoil it for them?